WRITING SHORT

Also by the authors of Life Writers

Turning Points: Life's Twists and Turns

WRITING SHORT

THE ART OF MICRO-MEMOIR

WITH A PREFACE BY PATRICIA CHARPENTIER

All grammatical and typographical errors have been
put in this book for your enjoyment in finding them.

Cover and interior design by Joan Keyes, Dovetail Publishing Services
Editing by Teresa TL Bruce
Proofreading by Etya Krichmar

ISBN-13: 978-1-939472-51-9

Published by LifeStory Publishing, a division of Writing Your Life
P.O. Box 541527
Orlando, Florida 32854
WritingYourLife.org

First Edition: May 2025
Printed in the USA
10 9 8 7 6 5 4 3 2

LIFESTORY
PUBLISHING

Dedication

To the authors of these amazing stories,
all the members of Life Writers,
and those everywhere who seek
to share their memories in writing.

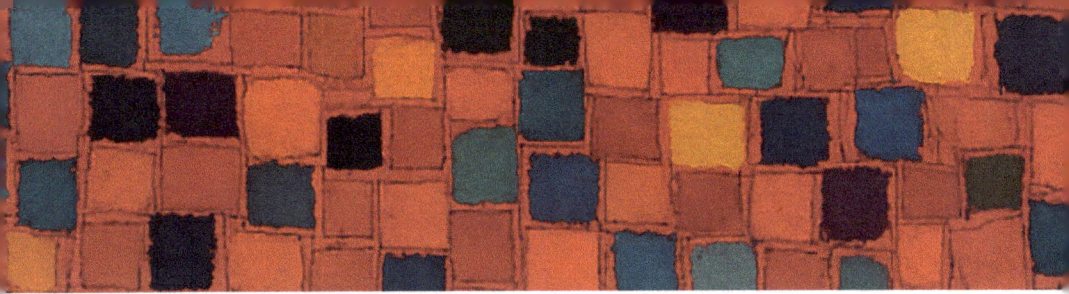

Contents

Preface

The Life Writers membership emerged from the COVID-19 lockdown—connecting life story writers from across the United States, Jamaica, Canada, and England in writing, reading, giving and receiving feedback, and befriending one another. What better way to celebrate Life Writers' fifth anniversary than with an anthology?

In the fall of 2024, our Life Writers spent four months studying *micro-memoir*, a genre of true stories defined by limited word count. The high end of *writing short*, often called *flash*, typically has a limit of 750–1,000 words.

By comparison, this collection, titled *Writing Short: The Art of Micro-Memoir*, focuses on true stories told in 300 words or less. That is the equivalent of just over one double-spaced page—not many words to tell a complete story. But the writers in this anthology did it.

The challenge involved selecting a topic and writing one to six micro-memoirs related to that subject using a maximum of 300 words each, including the little words like *a, an, in, of,* etc.

I joined in this project and never felt so frustrated in my writing life. Like many other Life Writers, my pieces started with 385 or 457 words, requiring dramatic cuts—an excellent exercise for all. We slashed sentences we loved to ensure every word counted.

In the following pages, you'll read stories about calling many places home and the home front of World War II, memorable pets and other animal encounters, beloved bicycles and motorcycle adventures, people and times we loved and others we'd rather forget, and many other slices of life.

You'll also discover the six-word memoir, made famous by *SMITH Magazine*, where stories must be told in exactly six words, not five, not seven.

Grab a cup of coffee or tea, and journey with us into the world of micro-memoir.

Patricia Charpentier
WritingYourLife.org
LifeWriters.us
298 Words

Clearing Spaces
Ricki Aiello

WALKING UP AND DOWN STAIRS

I walk up and down stairs more carefully these days. It isn't because I'm uncertain where my feet are or because my balance is impaired, but because I lost a friend, a sister of sorts. She fell and died in her home. Two short steps, a miscalculation, a slip perhaps, or her crutch tripped her up. No one knows for certain. The police made a wellness visit to her home and found her at the bottom of her cellar stairs on the concrete basement floor. She'd suffered a blow to the head. Marcia had been lying there for nearly two weeks.

I think about her when I'm climbing up and down my stairs. I think about how she died and the physical challenges she was forced to live with, a single crutch on every level of the condo, and the long climbs up and down to get from top to bottom and back again. But, I wonder, why do I think about how she died rather than how she lived? She was accomplished and learned. She cared about and for her sister without complaint.

I would want my friends and family to remember me by the way I lived my life, not how I died, especially if my death were as tragic as Marcia's. So now, when I climb my stairs up or down, I remember Marcia differently. I remember her courage, her fortitude, and her unwillingness to pity herself or accept the pity of others. I remember she was more than just someone who fell down a flight of stairs. She was a woman who learned how to climb the stairs in her life with determination and purpose. I hope I'm remembered in like manner.

"STOP THE MUSIC!"

My mother had little appreciation for music, but that didn't stop her from wanting to instill a musical interest in me. She enrolled me in a tap dancing class at age seven. I took two lessons, learned three steps, and begged to quit on day four.

I was in fifth grade when Mom decided I should take piano lessons. Playing piano appealed to me, but I soon found out that *playing piano* meant *practicing piano*.

Our piano was a beat-up old oak wooden upright. It sat in the partially finished downstairs basement, but our basement was scary, and I didn't like going down there. No ten-year-old girl wants to be in a moldy basement alone, surrounded by house-settling noises creaking and groaning around her. Then, there was the old boiler, pumping oil through the heating pipes. I was sure the ceiling and walls would fall onto and around me, and I would be covered by oil-soaked plaster.

The biggest problem with my musical attempts was my shyness. Piano, tap dancing, any activity meant I had to perform in front of others, not at all easy for someone like me. Years later, my ninety-year-old mother admitted she was shy too. Making friends in her life had never been easy for her, and performing in front of others, well, that would have been nearly impossible. We were more alike than I knew.

Now, I wish I had known about my mother's awkward growing up years when I was growing up. We might have found something we could share. I always thought Mom and I were two very different people. Maybe we weren't all that different, and perhaps if we'd had more time, we could have appreciated each other, grown closer, and not waited so long to say, "I love you."

"REALLY, GRAM?"

When I was a kid, weekends for my brother and me usually included visiting Gram's house in Wethersfield. I loved going to Gram's, and she loved to spoil us. Our visits were adventures as we explored Gram's pantry, looking for something sweet to eat. She was a fantastic cook and baker, raised in a Sicilian home in the old country. Gram's mom and aunts taught her the secrets of fine Italian flavors, which she readily shared with us, cooking or baking the most delightful and savory meals and treats. But, on occasion, we found something oddly out of place.

One day, my younger brother found a box of chocolate pudding. He couldn't read yet, but the picture on the box was a giveaway. He begged Gram to make it for us. I'd been around long enough to know Gram didn't like throwing anything away. She lived through two world wars and the Depression, and, in her mind, waste was a sin.

Not taking any chances, I looked closely at the box. Sure enough, printed on the back was the date, 1949, the year I was born. When I showed Gram the box, she laughed and said there were many old things in her house, but perhaps a ten-year-old box of pudding mix was too old.

Now I'm a grandmother, and like Gram, I don't like to waste anything. I have leftover candy from Halloween and Oreo cookies long past the expiration date. My grandchildren won't eat a thing before they check the date on the bag or the box, and they tease me just like I once teased my grandmother. Clearing out the spaces in our lives now and then isn't easy, but it makes room for something new.

OUTRUNNING MOM

I need some new bras. Mine are shabby and no longer up to the job. Replacing them means shopping, and I don't enjoy shopping. But I do need bras, ones that are comfortable and sized right for my changing shape.

As I grow older, I seem to have more of everything, though not always in the right places. I'm shorter, too. I used to be five feet, two inches tall. Not much, but more than I am now. My pants are too long; my shirt sleeves hang down past the palms of my hands, and, yes, my bras seem to be shrinking, though what they're covering isn't.

My dad was the one who alerted my mom to my growing needs. One day he said to her, "Vita, it might be time to get Ricki a bra."

Dutifully, my mom came home the next day, training bra in hand. She yanked the bra free from the shopping bag, pushing it toward me. "Try it on."

But I didn't want to, so I ran around the house with Mom close on my heels. I wasn't about to put that bra on.

I've worn a bra ever since, so I guess Mom won.

Over the years, I wondered why my father was the one to suggest a bra and not my mother. I don't believe my mother was negligent in her duties as a mom, but perhaps she, like me, didn't want time to pass so quickly. Maybe we were both running from the same thing, change. Of course, none of us can outrun what lies ahead, can we? It always seems to catch up with us. There would come a time when my mother didn't want to wear a bra, and I was the one chasing her, bra in hand.

BIRD IN HAND

A few years ago, I visited my cousin on a warm autumn day. I rang the bell and waited. Hearing a high-pitched chirp behind

Ricki Aiello

me, I turned to look. A tiny baby finch with soft gray-and-white feathers and a pale beak sat on the lower step. The little bird seemed puffed up with pride at its achievement but unsure of its next move. Surprised to see the baby so near, I held my hand out, palm down, and softly said, "Hi, little one. Where did you come from?" Without hesitation, the bird fluttered over my hand and landed, its tiny claws gripping my flesh.

We stood perfectly still, staring at one another, neither believing the situation nor knowing what to do next. The spell broke when Mama Bird settled on the lawn in front of the scene, squawking vigorously at her offspring—and probably at me too. I didn't know what she was saying, but I got the gist, and so did the little bird. With a clumsy lift of wings and body, the baby tested the air, fluttered above me, and flew off to be with its mom.

Growing up, I remember the many times I heard the insistent voice of my mother calling me home, "Ricki, come here right now." And I did. Like every little kid, I was learning to stretch my wings and fly too, but when my mother called me home, I listened.

As a mother now, I know what it's like to want to protect your children no matter their age, to watch over them and not have them fly too close to danger. My mother wasn't ready to let me fly alone. The mama bird wasn't ready to let her baby go. Soon, perhaps, but not yet.

THE OLD RED LEATHER RECLINER

Most mornings, I begin my day with a cup of tea, meditation and prayer, and a freshly fed dog sitting at my feet. The old red leather chair suits us both. I bought the recliner in 2013 to replace the one my mother had to leave behind when we moved her from Virginia to Connecticut. She was unhappy about the move, but age, health, and repeated falls made the decision necessary.

The chair occupied much of the space in Mom's small studio apartment. It became a place where she could eat, sleep, and watch the endless hours of her favorite detective series, Monk. Cranberry red, motorized to lift her into position, easy access to the simple round disc split in half with a sliced groove just below the right armrest to maneuver up, down, forward, and back, the chair and Mom were comfortable roommates for all of nine months. By that time, she had fallen again, and more than once. She ended up in the hospital and nearly died.

Once again, a move was necessary, this time to a nursing home. Little by little, my mother's world shrunk, but the red leather chair didn't. It was too big for her new residence, so the chair came home to me.

Now, twelve years later, it is wearing out, the motor sluggish and uncooperative. A physically lumbering piece of life shuttering to its own end, like my mother in those last days before she died. I considered replacing the old thing, but it is comfortable and comforting, a reminder of my mother. Another connection I don't want to sever, a reminder of better times and the inevitability of aging, something I'm slowly learning to grow into, just as my mother had to.

RICKI AIELLO

Ricki Aiello is a New England writer. After retiring from full-time ministry, she wanted to explore creative writing. With that in mind, she took her first writing class in 2016 and has enrolled in many since. Her publications include personal essays in *Front Porch Review*, nonfiction devotional pieces in *The Upper Room* and *Christian Century*, and a short story titled "Remember When" featured in the literary magazine *Portrait of New England*. Additionally, one of her poems has been accepted for inclusion in an anthology published by *Tiferet Journal*. Currently, she is focusing on memoir essays that explore her relationship with her mother.

Beyond Ricki's writing pursuits, she has a passion for reading across various genres, with a particular affinity for memoir and poetry, though she also appreciates a well-crafted mystery.

Becoming Me

Norma Beasley

THE ART OF SOUND

In September 2018, Patricia Charpentier introduced our writing class to a new experience at the Orlando Museum of Art. We attended the exhibition of Nick Cave, best known for wearable mixed media constructions known as *Soundsuits*, which act simultaneously as fashion, sculpture, and noisemaking performance art. Our assignment: tour the exhibit and document our physical, spiritual, visual, and mental impressions of the displays for a possible narrative.

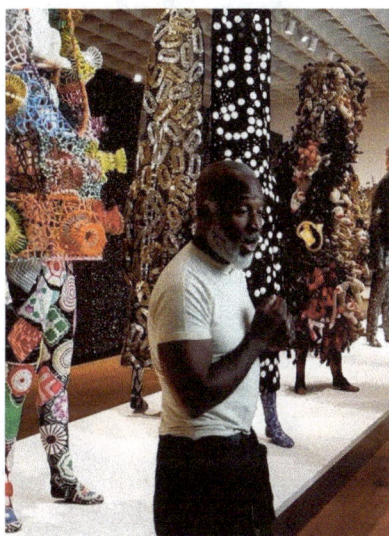

Nick Cave

Soundsuits originated as metaphorical suits of armor in response to the Rodney King beatings and have evolved into vehicles for empowerment. Fully concealing the body, the *Soundsuits* serve as an alien second skin that obscures race, gender, and class, allowing viewers to look without bias toward the wearer's identity. Cave's sculptures are crafted in collaboration with artisans using a dizzying array of materials that include beads, raffia, buttons, sequins, twigs, fur, ceramic figurines, toys, and fabric. The

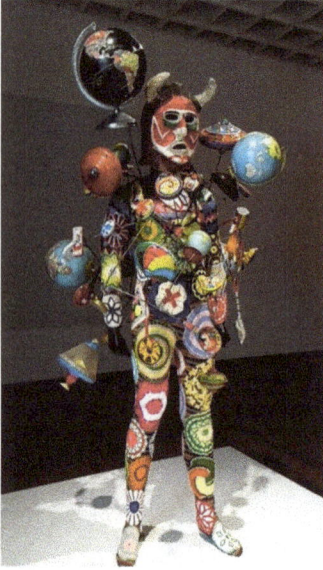

Soundsuits are also displayed in exhibitions as static sculptures, sometimes arranged as groups of figures that are striking in their diversity and powerful stance. Cave's structures also include nonfigurative assemblages, intricate arrangements of found objects that project out from the wall, and installations enveloping entire rooms. Cave draws design inspiration from a variety of sources, including West African sacred dress, natural landscapes, antique shops, flea markets, and handcrafts.

Throughout his career, Cave made use of found and ready-made materials to reference cultural and autobiographical issues. The *Soundsuits* are named for the sounds made

when worn by performers. Their meaning shifts and multiplies with each exhibition and performance, set in places as varied as a theater stage, fashion runway, and city street. He also transforms painful experiences into hopeful images.

LET'S BE FRIENDS FOREVER

We connected through a third party, Pearl and me. We were fraternal members of the Rosicrucian Order, AMORC, and each wanted to travel to San Jose, California, for a convention and needed a roommate.

"Why don't you contact Pearl," said Ras, the group leader in Brooklyn.

"Who is Pearl?" I asked.

"You know. The new member with salt-and-pepper hair. She carries herself with dignity."

"Oh, yeah, I know who you mean. I noticed her too." We connected and made it to the convention. Thus began a friendship of thirty-plus years.

I'm a hillbilly from West Virginia, born and bred on chicken, brains, burgers, and taters. Pearl, a native of Barbados, experienced beautiful beaches, aquamarine waters, and rolling hills. She introduced me to a different but delicate palette of Bajan foods: flying fish and *cou cou*, the national dish; sweet black cake made of prunes, cherries, and raisins, and soaked in rum, served at Christmastime; sorrel, a dark red drink spiked with rum, also enjoyed during the holidays; souse, which is pickled pork; fish cakes made of salted cod or whitefish; hot pepper sauce; plantains; ginger beer; maubey, a bitter drink that made my tongue curl; roti, a filled burrito with potatoes, veggies, and chicken, fish, or beef; and breadfruit. Yum-yum.

We became best buds while world-traveling. Naramata, British Columbia. Sweden. Copenhagen. England. Egypt. Jamaica. Canada. Barbados, twice.

Pearl became a branch manager with Chase Bank. She also loved horse racing and often won when betting; she knew all the horses by name, their racing records, and the jockeys who rode them. She taught me how to reconcile my bank statements. Became my mom, confidant, and big sis.

While visiting one day, Pearl said, "Let's be friends forever." And so it was until she passed away.

Pearl

FROM PENCIL TO PIXEL

The seeds of our becoming are sown long before our arrival on this earth plane. Our progenitors usually influence our choices toward self-realization. Since I lost both parents before the age of three, you might wonder what propelled me along the path I chose. My only clue was that I had been told my dad loved to doodle. Howdy Doody coloring books, paint-by-number kits, and a Draw Me contest furthered my interest in art. Winning school poster contests, receiving the Downes Award in high school as an outstanding artist, and capturing a National Scholastic Award was a prestigious confirmation for a creative teen.

I taught summer school art classes as I earned a BA degree from West Virginia University. Summer school prepared me for a salaried position at Armstrong High School in Richmond, Virginia. But teaching in an urban setting was not to my liking. I was a Yankee at heart in the Deep South—unaccustomed to addressing problems in underserved communities and underperforming students. I relocated to New York and earned an MFA degree from Pratt Institute.

At Pratt, I studied under George McNeil, embracing abstract expressionism, a movement that reflected his free, figurative expressionism. He ignited something inside me that I didn't know existed. Then he said, "I have no more to teach you."

I had arrived as a fine artist.

Finally, I found my true calling at Harcourt Brace & World, renowned educational publishers who hired me as an art editor. Eventually, I became the company's first Black managing art director in the digital age under the tutelage of Joe Loughman. I retired in 2003 in Orlando, Florida. My journey was complete.

Looking back, I believe the hand of God guided me every step of the way. Through thick and thin.

MY SPIRITUAL JOURNEY

I was introduced to Sunday school and church as a youngster by my grandparents, who were deeply committed Christians. Services were attended every Sunday. A hiatus ensued after graduating from high school.

The thought-provoking Rosicrucian ad below caught my attention one day as I browsed through a *Psychology Today* magazine. The illustration was arcane to me at the time. The verbiage piqued my curiosity and ignited my desire to learn more about the powers of mind and the Rosicrucian Order, AMORC.

I couldn't afford membership dues but had access to the *Rosicrucian Digest*. This periodical became my bible. The

THOUGHTS HAVE WINGS
You Can Influence Others
With Your Thinking!

Rosicrucian Order, AMORC

concept of the "master within" was embraced even though I didn't understand its meaning. I joined the Order, became a lodge member, then lodge secretary. I came to know a respected organization while seizing the opportunity to evolve personally and spiritually.

A principal edict espoused by the Order is to give service. I have been an officer in administrative and ritualistic positions; I'm currently serving my second four-year term as district manager in Florida.

I have learned to honor the divinity in each person I meet to the best of my ability, including children, and have tried to never cast disparaging remarks toward anyone. Taking the high road or remedying the situation, if possible, is my goal.

I have enjoyed the opportunity to participate in world, national, and local conventions, workshops, initiations, teleconferences, book salon discussions, convocations, and mystical weekends.

The Order's monographs, a study syllabus, have been invaluable in learning about principles, techniques, and experiments in mysticism. The *Digest* and *Forum* have added to my enlightenment. Access to other resources includes the Council of Solace, Rosicrucian TV, and free downloadable books.

Being a Rosicrucian has become a way of life, a living philosophy of pragmatic mysticism.

THE GAME ISN'T OVER UNTIL IT'S OVER
October 3, 1951

I am ten years old, living with my grandparents, Eugene and Leiugania Dooms, attracted to baseball because Jackie Robinson has been hired by the Brooklyn Dodgers. The first Black athlete to break the color barrier in Major League Baseball.

I become a Dodger fan. Ross Hodges, a play-by-play baseball announcer, is calling the final third game of a three-game playoff between the Dodgers and the New York Giants.

I am biting my nails. Gritting my teeth. Nervously pumping my legs up and down. *We got this. Ninth inning. Dodgers lead 4–2.*

The radio call sounds something like this:

"Bobby Thompson . . . Up there swinging . . . Branca throws . . ."

Crack! The bat hit the ball.

"There's a long drive . . . It's gonna be, I believe . . . The Giants won the pennant! The Giants won the pennant! The Giants won the pennant! The Giants won the pennant! Bobby Thompson hits into the lower deck of the left field stands! The Giants win the pennant, and they're goin' crazy—they're goin' crazy. Hey-oh! I don't believe it. I don't believe it! I don't believe it! Bobby Thompson . . . hit a line drive . . . into the lower deck . . . of the left field stands . . . And this blame place is goin' crazy! Horace

Stoneham has got a winner! The Giants won it . . . by a score of five to four . . . And they're pickin' Bobby Thompson up . . . and carryin' him off the field!"[1]

I turn the radio off. Dumbfounded. Go outside and sit on my front porch steps. I can't believe it. The Giants won the pennant.

My neighbor, Peggy Chapell passes by and looks at my face. "What happened?"

"Nothin'!" I yell. Still stunned.

It taught me a lesson—not to think the game is over until it is over.

BAZOOKA

Donnie D., a childhood schoolmate of mine, and I were fierce competitors playing badminton. We both loved the drop shot, a shot hit relatively soft, to land just over and close to the net—most of the time, impossible to return. I relished seeing him gallop to the net to return the shot. He always entangled himself in the net, losing the point. The competitiveness carried over into a tabletop pinball game called Bazooka during the 1950s.

Bazooka was a game of chance rather than one of skill, developed by Marx, a toy company. The game, a self-contained unit, consisted of five colored marbles, scored anchors that captured the glass balls as they rolled down an inclined plane, and a spring trigger that released each marble toward a target. Highest score was the winner. We agreed not to influence gravity as each marble rolled down the incline toward a target. During the game, we were joined by my cousin Anita, who wanted to watch us play.

---

[1] https://en.wikipedia.org/wiki/Russ_Hodges

Donnie shot his marbles first and accumulated a high score.

Now it was my turn. Lady Luck wasn't with me, and I became anxious and frustrated.

Anita made it worse by teasing me. "Nah-nah-nah-nah-nah-nah," she chimed, while using the shame-shame finger gesture.

"Shut up," I yelled. "Leave me alone. You're not playing this game."

The taunts continued. Suddenly, I sprang to my feet, attacked her, and knocked her to the ground with me on top, breaking my glasses. Grandma heard the ruckus and came outside to see what was going on. She sent Anita home and made me come inside. Donnie ran away. Grandma threw the game in the garbage.

Anita and I, now in our eighties, never fought again.

NORMA BEASLEY

Norma Beasley is from the "Wild and Wonderful" state of West Virginia.

She graduated from the University of West Virginia with a BA in art and from the Pratt Institute in New York with an MFA degree.

In 2003, Norma retired as a managing art director after thirty-five years of service with Harcourt Inc., an elementary education publisher specializing in curriculum development embracing the disciplines of math, reading, science, social studies, history, and health.

In 2019, the Florida Writer's Association (FWA) selected her memoir *Living Inside Out* as a semifinalist in the annual Royal Palm Literary Awards competition. The Florida Authors and Publishers Association awarded the memoir first place for cover design in 2020. Norma has written for FWA, the *Orlando Sentinel*, and the Rosicrucian Order, AMORC.

Norma also enjoys gardening, sports, photography, and travel.

Bolting Toward the Edge

Patricia Charpentier

FRIDAY NIGHT RIDE

I had no interest in Ed, the veterinarian, until he said he owned two horses. With only a fringe of dark hair encircling his bald head, he had a big nose and laughed in a strange, snorting kind of way. But he had horses, and I loved horses even though I spent little time on or around them.

I'd begged my parents for a horse for years. A family friend even wanted to give me a purebred Appaloosa pony, but my parents didn't believe I'd care for it once the real work began. They were probably right. So whenever a horse opportunity presented itself, I jumped on it.

The timing was right for a distraction, especially the equine kind. I had been in a mentally and emotionally abusive affair with Mark for eighteen months. We worked together but, thankfully, not in the same building. He was married and had two teenage kids. I knew being with him was wrong on many levels, but I couldn't pull myself away. I ended it a hundred times and then ran back for more. He was my heroin in human form.

Again, I repeated what I had always done with relationships—tumble into a new one to get me out of the old one. I had done that since I was thirteen years old. I was thirty-five now.

When Ed asked if I wanted to go for a ride after work on Friday, May 3, 1991, I leaped at the chance. I had not seen or talked to Mark in eight days, the longest since the affair started. I was in painful physical withdrawal. I couldn't stop crying—couldn't think or eat or sleep. I needed a distraction, and Ed and his horses seemed the perfect solution.

UNBRIDLED FEAR

I don my jeans, boots, and straw hat from my *Urban Cowboy* days, and Ed and I drive to where he boards his two polo horses, Flash and PK.

Ed saddles the horses and cups his hands to help me onto Flash because the top of my head barely reaches the horses' muzzles. Once I situate myself on the tiny English saddle, Ed says, "Hang out here. I'll run PK. Then, we'll switch." He wipes his sweaty, too-tall forehead and races PK across the pasture for the next twenty minutes.

I still feel tight, on edge, but I breathe deeply, taking in the comingled scents of horse, grass, and manure, telling myself, *You're okay. Relax.*

Ed comes back, hoists me onto PK, and I begin to cry.

"Aw, you're good," he says, patting my leg. "Just walk PK, cool him off, and we'll go for a nice ride, okay?" With that, he speeds off on Flash.

PK breathes hard, snorts, and refuses to walk. He takes two steps, stops, shakes his head.

I cry harder, feeling alone and scared without Mark.

PK begins trotting, bouncing me in the saddle. I try to stop him, but he picks up speed. I yell for Ed, pull on the reins, but PK runs even faster. I scream and sob, try to hold on but soon lose the reins, and grab his mane as he bolts toward the barn.

Ahead, I see the fencing PK needs to wind us through, so I force myself to calm down and talk to him. I lose my grip as we approach the first open gate and slam into the post. The impact tosses me back across the horse. I fall to the left, but my boot catches in the stirrup.

Finally, I hit the ground. PK keeps running.

BARELY BREATHING

Two men I don't recognize look down at me as I lie in the dirt. When we'd arrived, the sky was blue, the pasture green. Now, all I see are shades of gray.

I hear hoofbeats behind me, and Ed joins the men staring down at me. They talk as if I'm not there.

"What happened?" one asks.

"I'm not sure," Ed says. "I heard her scream. I got close but didn't try to stop them. I didn't want to spook PK even more."

Pain radiates throughout my entire body. I can't breathe. I suck in shallow, rapid bites of air and taste blood in my mouth.

"Can you move your feet?" Ed asks. I focus all my energy, and my right boot moves a half inch. "That's good."

"What will you do with her?" one man asks.

"I'll take her to my house and watch her," Ed says. "If she gets worse, I'll bring her to the hospital. Grab her legs. Help me get her to my car."

Pain rockets through all parts of my body as they carry me to Ed's car and slide me across the back seat. I smell Ed's golden retriever, Jake, in the cushion covered with dog hair.

Ed drives with one arm over the back seat to keep me from rolling onto the floorboard. Each bump he hits sends shock waves through my body. "Sorry," he says after each bounce. He talks to me, telling me I'm okay.

But I'm not okay. I can't pull in enough air. I hear soft moaning, and it takes me a moment to realize it's coming from deep inside my chest. It soothes me.

A half-hour later, Ed makes a hard right turn and says, "Hang on. We're going to the hospital."

IN THE ER

"We're here," Ed says as he sits on the horn and jumps out of the car.

Moments later, the car doors fly open. A woman dressed in white looks down on me. "Oh, sweetie. We're going to take care of you." She puts her warm hand on my forehead.

"Get a backboard," she says to the guy looking at me from the other opened door, and he disappears.

She continues to talk to me until several others show up. One fastens a brace around my neck; the others slide a rigid yellow board onto the seat next to me.

"Sweetie, we need to put this under you." I nod. My body screams with every tug and bump.

Behind me, I hear her yell at Ed, "What the hell were you thinking, bringing her in like this? Are you crazy?"

Ed doesn't respond.

"Stay here," she tells him as they push me through double doors into a large room filled with light and noise and people.

"We'll take good care of you," she tells me.

People rush around me, cut off my clothes, start an IV, hook me up to monitors, place a mask over my nose and mouth.

A young guy in a white coat rushes in. "Hi, Patricia. I'm Dr. Samuels. You've taken quite a tumble, haven't you?" I try to nod. "Your right lung is collapsed. That's why you're having a hard time breathing. I can fix it, but it's going to hurt."

With that, he makes a small cut on my side and pushes hard to insert a plastic tube into my chest cavity. The pain is horrible, but I hear a whooshing sound and take a deep breath, the first in a while. "Good. Now, we'll get you something for pain and check you out."

QUIET IN THE CHAOS

I watch nurses and doctors run in and out, each with a distinct purpose to fulfill.

"Gotta take her upstairs," a guy with short gray hair and glasses says. I hear the click as he unlocks the brakes, and I groan as he shoves the gurney forward.

As I roll by, the nurse with kind green eyes says, "I'll be waiting for you when you come back." I manage a slight smile.

Other orderlies wheel me around the hospital, where I'm imaged, scanned, and x-rayed. After each trip, they return me to the curtained-off room with the same nurse. She seems glad to see me every time.

This nurse remains close by, checks the IVs in both arms, hangs new bags, and studies the machines I can hear behind me but cannot see. I watch as she jots notes in a folder that grows larger by the minute with what I assume are test results. I listen to the rhythm of my heart beating on one of the monitors, a steady *blip, blip, blip,* and feel soothed.

At one point, there's a lull when the medical team isn't rushing around. The noise around me dims, and a blanket of silence falls over me. I feel quiet inside. Why, I'm not sure, but I feel calm.

I see everything around me from a distance, but I'm not afraid. I wonder, *Am I going to live, or am I going to die?* I don't know the answer, but I am okay either way. I am more curious about how this will turn out for me.

The moment is interrupted by another trip to somewhere to have some other test done. That perspective doesn't return, but the feeling stays with me.

RELIEF AND FAILURE

"My left ankle hurts," I tell the nurse during a brief lull in the frantic action surrounding me.

"I'll need to cut off your boot to check it out." I didn't realize all my clothes had been cut off, but they left my boots on.

"No, I love these boots."

"I can take it off, but it will hurt if something is wrong." I nod. In one swift motion, she cups the heel and pulls. I nearly pass out from the pain as I hear her yell, "Get ortho in here."

I look down. My leg faces forward, but my foot is horizontal, pointing to the left.

The nurse with kind eyes stays with me. She acknowledges I came in with *that guy* but asks if she should call anyone else.

"Denise, please," and I give her the number. Denise is my only real friend. Living secretly in an affair has made my life small, without much room for people.

Denise shows up soon afterward. "Hey there," she says and kisses me on the forehead. "How are you doing?"

"Been better," I say. Even though I can breathe now, talking takes effort I don't have.

"I bet." Denise, also a nurse, talks with the woman who's remained by my side and learns where I am medically.

Before being ushered out, Denise asks, "Do you want me to call Mark?"

"I don't know." She knows the pain I've been in, extracting myself from this affair. "Should I?"

She nods. "Yeah, I think he needs to know."

"Go ahead."

Seemingly within minutes, Mark is by my bedside in the ER. "I'm here now, baby. You're going to be okay. I'm here."

I believe him and feel both relief and failure. I've opened the door yet again.

PATRICIA CHARPENTIER

Patricia Charpentier is a Cajun from South Louisiana and a long-time editor, ghostwriter, and instructor. She has been writing for publication since she was fourteen years old and is currently working on a memoir about how the accident described in this series changed the rest of her life. Eventually, Patricia's twenty-six broken bones and other injuries healed, and she ultimately ended that destructive affair for the last time. But it would take years of counseling and participation in two recovery programs for her to learn to live—and love—in a healthy way.

Patricia resides in Orlando, Florida, with her sweet husband, Bob. You can read more about her work on her websites, WritingYourLife.org and LifeWriters.us.

Bicycles

Raquel David

UNCLE ARTHUR'S WORKSHOP

Uncle Arthur, a hardworking immigrant from Portugal, worked by day for someone else as a mechanic, but after hours, he worked for himself, building and repairing bikes. Saturday mornings, I'd follow Arthur to his workroom, down the poorly lit, steep staircase. At the bottom of the steps, a massive workbench dominated the shop. The height of the table came to my nose, so I could see an array of Allen wrenches, screws, and screwdrivers. Off to the shadows, seven to eight cycles —either fully repaired or awaiting help—neatly stood in a straight line on their kickstands, equidistant apart.

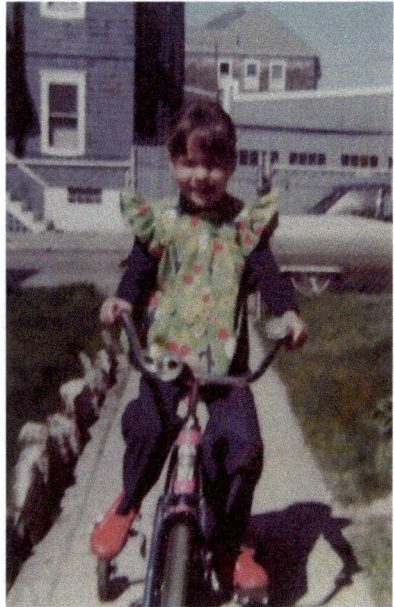

Raquel David, riding the bicycle Uncle Arthur made for her

Three feet from the work surface, and up one step, shone a brightly lit office. This narrow room housed handlebars, frames, seats, pedals, and wheels.

I trailed my uncle as he meandered through his shop, careful not to touch much of anything because I disliked getting dirty,

27

and while everything was neat and organized, it was most definitely a workingman's shop.

Out of this shadowy, stuffy workplace, Arthur crafted the most splendid two-wheeler for me. Well, actually, it had four wheels, but not for long. This soon-to-be two-wheeler fit my four-year-old frame perfectly. Its purple body came equipped with a banana seat and a white basket for holding trinkets.

I practiced riding my new bike along the cement path connecting our back porch to the front gate. Soon, I was pedaling past the gate and along Stapleton Street, with handlebar streamers blowing in the wind.

THE STATION HOUSE

I sang the theme song to my favorite show, *Zoom*. I laughed. I talked to myself. I rode in circles. I could do all these things, yet there was one thing I could not do. Should not do. Was told not to do. And that was, ride to the police station at the end of our street.

The station house was off-limits. Dangerous people hung out there.

Riding in circles got boring. The police station had a bubbler, carved out of granite, and I wanted to drink from it.

After supper one night, I headed west on Stapleton Street with the sun in my eyes, legs pedaling as fast as they could in the direction of the forbidden police station.

Raquel David, riding her bicycle along Stapelton Street, New Bedford, Massachusetts

Reaching the precinct, a single-story, yellow-brick building, I sat back on my banana seat, let my small sandaled feet touch the pavement, and gazed up at the imposing vertical columns flanking the entrance to the station.

I felt small. Small and scared. *Is one of those bad people my parents told me about going to snatch me?*

I glimpsed the bubbler but lost my desire to drink from it.

I turned around and pedaled the short distance back to my house—where I saw my mom and dad standing with their arms crossed over their chests. Their lips were tight, straight horizontal lines across their faces.

Maybe, I negotiated with myself, *they didn't see anything.*

Oh, but they had.

Worse than the light spanking I got was seeing the disappointed look on their faces. I vowed never to go back to the police station. Instead, I learned how to make figure eights.

THE SALES LEADERSHIP CLUB

I really wanted a ten-speed, Schwinn bicycle.

If I earned half the money for the Schwinn, my parents would pitch in the rest.

But how? I didn't receive an allowance. My sister and I did chores because it was expected.

Most afternoons, I'd perch on the front porch reading mystery books, clinging to the clues as I sought to solve the puzzles. And it was a puzzle how I would earn the money for the Schwinn.

One afternoon when the postman arrived, he handed me a pile of mail. Among this assortment was a large white envelope from The Sales Leadership Club in Springfield, Massachusetts. This held intrigue.

My parents and I sorted through the envelope's contents on the kitchen table. "Please read carefully. Important notice to customers. Satisfaction guaranteed. Thank you for your order." Gosh, this all sounded so consequential.

The Sales Leadership Club wanted salespeople to sell their products. They guaranteed shopper satisfaction with their Christmas cards: "Christmas Favorites, 40 personalized cards with envelopes for only $3.25."

This was something I could get behind. Christmas was my favorite holiday, plus I had the whole summer to sell. I don't remember how many cards I needed to sell, but it was in the hundreds.

"Sure you want to do this?" my dad quietly asked.

I nodded my head up and down vigorously.

"It's going to be hot, and honey, just so you know, not everyone will want to buy Christmas cards in July," my mom gently added.

"I can do it. I can do it," I sang.

For my first day on the job, I selected shorts from my bureau, braided my hair, and attached matching yarn ribbons. I set out that day energized at the prospect of selling enough cards to purchase my future bike.

I'LL LOOK FOR YOU ON YOUR BIKE

The Henaults, across the street, were my first stop. Henry and Mary were friendly with my parents. Choosing them as my first potential customers was sensible. Mrs. Hart was next. Her youngest son, Jimmy, and I were in the same grade. When we were little, my mom sometimes watched Jimmy at our house after morning kindergarten. Now, I made my way through the neighborhood, knocking on familiar doors with familiar faces and with frequent success.

For my final sales call, I rang the Blaines' doorbell. Mrs. Blaine appeared on the other side of the screen door with a fixed look that stated, "What the heck do you want?"

I made my brief pitch. "Would you like to buy some Christmas cards?"

She delayed a second before letting me in. "Why are you selling Christmas Cards?" she asked bluntly.

"I want to buy a bike."

"Humph," she responded. The woman of the house plopped onto the paisley-patterned sofa positioned near the babbling television, moistened her fingertip with the tip of her tongue, and took her time going through the glossy catalog, pausing at every page to inspect the greeting cards. She intermittently looked up to check on her "stories" before returning to the catalog. This no-frills lady, to my delight, settled on two sets of deluxe Christmas cards.

The late-afternoon sun warmed my shoulders as I emerged from the Blaine's house. I started down the front steps when I heard, "Hold on a sec." Mrs. Blaine held out a pen I left behind and whispered, "Good luck, Raquel. I'll look for you on your bike."

FALLING IN LOVE

The smell of rubber hit me as we entered the bike shop. Hundreds of bicycles—some upright, some parked on a thirty-degree incline, and several dismantled or upside down being repaired—encircled me.

After speaking with the salesman, dressed in a smart plaid suit, an associate carefully wheeled a brilliant red ten-speed out to me.

Leveling the seat, adjusting the height so my knee was bent just so, and ensuring the handlebar position was comfortable,

I was then encouraged to ride the bike around the parking lot. Straddling the sloped front bar of this magnificent two-wheeler, I pushed off the pavement with my right foot, started gliding, then pedaled along. The tires were skinny, designed for speed and endurance. I settled onto the bike's narrow seat and thought, *Whoa, this is going to take some getting used to.*

Talking about getting used to something, let's mention the drop handlebars. They looked great, especially wrapped in white tape, but the positioning had my body leaning forward at a precarious seventy-degree angle, and this was while holding onto the top part of the handlebar. The crucial brakes were attached to these handles, so I didn't have much of a choice. Keeping true to my conservative nature, I wouldn't attempt the more aggressive drop brakes for a while.

I rode the distance of the parking lot, turned the bicycle around, and returned to my starting point with relative ease.

Back inside the shop, I purchased an accessory of sorts, a small container of red Schwinn paint. This was essential for retouching scratches, thereby keeping my bike looking brand-new. I was attached to my new purchase and embraced it like a loving parent. Little did I know, my inner mamma bear was about to awaken.

MAMA BEAR

Now, how to get the bike home? All four of us with a ten-speed bike would never fit in the family Corolla. However, my parents had a clever plan to break bad news to me at the last minute.

My father would be riding my bike home. MY BIKE! So unfair. I was frustrated by the situation but realized there was little else to be done. I would have to see this setback through to the end.

Now, I love my dad. He made coffee milkshakes and egg salad sandwiches for the neighborhood kids when Mom worked second shift. He let my sister and me sit in his J. R. Ewing chair at work and spin in circles. Occasionally, he'd run to the corner store after supper but before bedtime and bring home a rich, decadent chocolate Swiss roll, which we quickly devoured.

Here's what bothered me: My dad was terribly messy. Papers were scattered about. Coffee mugs left in every room. Socks by the couch. He thrived on chaos and wasn't easily rattled.

I thrived on order. Good thing I bought the paint. As a spindly ten-year-old—"a long drink of water," some would say—I was bothered, worried my dad's girth would ruin my bike. Would those skinny tires even make it? I wasn't even sure my dad could ride a bike.

Just after lunch, Dad arrived home, hair matted to the top of his curly head, breathing slightly elevated. And with the biggest smile, he proclaimed. "She's all yours."

My bike looked perfect.

"Thanks, Dad," I answered. This mama bear had nothing to worry about. Her baby was safely home.

RAQUEL DAVID

Raquel David is a retired fifth-grade teacher from Somerset, Massachusetts. She taught her students all the subject areas for twenty years and is currently working on her first micro-memoir, titled "Bicycles." Raquel is interested in reading memoirs, biographies, and historical fiction. She lives in The Villages, Florida, with her husband, Peter. She enjoys cooking, traveling, bike riding, race-walking, ballet, going to concerts, the theatre, reading, swimming, and playing mah-jongg.

Divine Intervention: Merited or Unmerited Favor

Lorna Deane

UNEXPECTED

I gazed at the stark white walls of my hospital room, affording me a better view than of tubes and other devices connected to my body. I was in Trinidad, recovering from pelvic surgery. The chief nurse—matron—had just left after completing her morning rounds. Her visits, pleasantries, and encouraging words lifted my spirits.

Sometime later, my sister, Pauline, who flew down from Jamaica, arrived. I recounted that after pelvic surgery, I developed small bowel ileus, leading to an extended stay in the hospital. There seemed no clear treatment options.

She shared with me updates on the status of my family in Jamaica, and of Khalil, my younger son, who was at home with my husband. Her presence was comforting.

Soon, I began to tire, but I tried to keep awake. Pauline noticed and said, "It seems we have chatted long enough. Let me read from the book of Psalms for you."

Shortly after she started reading, my telephone rang. I answered softly, "Hello."

A male voice responded. It was Reverend Bompart from my local Church of the Nazarene, St. James. He said, "Lorna,

I've been thinking about you. I realize I have not seen or heard from you for some time. I had to call you today. Khalil told me where you are. How are you? Nothing serious, I hope."

"I hope so too," I answered.

"I understand your sister is there. Would you like me to read a psalm for you and then pray with you?"

"Please do," I whispered.

He read from Psalm 121. The identical chapter Pauline had begun to read.

Stunned, I grappled with what had just happened. Was this mere coincidence? What prompted Reverend Bompart to call me when he did? What led him to choose that identical passage of Scripture?

LIFE-SAVING IMPACT OF A DREAM

Fourteen days passed since I entered the hospital for pelvic surgery and a projected five-day stay. My medical team now included my nephew, a heart specialist in Louisville, Kentucky. He took charge of my case. My surgeon consulted with him daily.

A second surgery was contemplated. This proved not viable. My options narrowed. I told my sister, Pauline, my wishes, details of my finances, and the location of titles to my worldly possessions.

Nightly sleep eluded me. Staff arriving for their midnight rounds to record my vitals found me wide-awake and talking.

However, just before dawn, I fell into a dream-filled sleep. The chief nurse—matron—and her assistant both looked forward to hearing my dreams. Each morning, I recounted an action-filled adventure with vivid details of places and people I encountered.

One night was different. I dreamed I was surrounded by several stick figures. Alarmed, in fear I recoiled. *These must* be demons. *I don't know how to fight demons.* Teachings from my Christian faith surged into memory: *At the name of Jesus, demons fear and tremble.* I cried out, "The blood of Jesus. The blood of Jesus!"

The following morning, unsettled, I shared my dream with the matron. Then, I experienced a burning craving and made a request. "May I have some ginger tea, please?"

Up until then, since the day after my surgery, I could not eat or drink.

The matron brought the tea and assisted me in sipping it. Within a couple of hours, the matron observed that my symptoms had begun to resolve.

Three days later, I was discharged from the hospital. The smile on the matron's face reflected love and relief. She left the reception area, hugged me, and whispered, "After I heard your last dream, I knew you would get well."

FORESHADOWING

In 1990, after extended sick leave, I returned to the Central Bank of Trinidad and Tobago. Due to legislative changes, my position in the Exchange Control Department, the ECD, was eliminated. I learned I was promoted to a newly created position in the governor's office. This required a new workspace. On the governor's instructions, the vacant deputy governor's office was prepared for me.

Observer at Conference of Regional Deputy Governors, El Salvador, 1992

I felt honored.

Was this experience foreshadowed years before?

એ

It happened in 1979, one year after I moved from Jamaica and commenced working in the ECD of the Central Bank of Trinidad and Tobago. I felt apprehensive when I was summoned to the governor's office. At that time, the executive area, including his office, was restricted and referred to by staff as "the red carpet."

I took in the imposing figure of the governor and thought, *His office and authority sit well on him.* That explained, partially, why he was respected by all, feared by a few.

After enquiring about the welfare of my family and me, he said, "Mrs. Deane, I am expecting two gentlemen from Company X[2] at 2:00 p.m. They require advice on exchange control matters. I selected you to meet with them."

I listened, puzzled.

He continued. "I am confident you can conduct the meeting. Please use the deputy governor's office, next to mine."

This was unheard of.

&

Eleven years separated these events.

- The 1979 governor retired in 1984.
- His successor completed construction of the Twin Towers, the tallest buildings in the Caribbean then. The Central Bank relocated to one of these towers in 1986.
- The executive area had an office for the governor and two for deputy governors, though only one was appointed.
- In 1990, a third governor held office.

---

[2] The name of the prominent "Company X" has been omitted.

SECOND CHANCES

I remember hearing my dad say, "You will never get a second bite of that cherry."

Over the years, as I mulled over his wise words, my interpretation grew more nuanced, and I internalized it as "Opportunities lost might never return."

Some opportunities represented pivotal moments, and the choices I exercised had a significant influence on the trajectory of my life. The opportunities I allowed to pass by, faded into oblivion.

Or did they?

Two such opportunities come to mind. The first arose in 1968 at the University of Manitoba. I was selected to be among a group of undergraduates who would be mentored to pursue postgraduate studies in economic development. I declined and held steadfast to my plan to return to Jamaica as soon as possible.

The second pivotal opportunity occurred in 1970. One of my high school teachers visited Dad after I graduated and said, "Mr. Gibson, congratulations on Lorna's success. She must not stop there but go on to read for a master's degree in English. If finances are an issue, I will assist."

I did not give the offer serious consideration. An early return to Jamaica remained my priority.

I am satisfied with my life journey, firm in my belief that my experiences were consequences of choices I made. I also faced and navigated the vicissitudes life inevitably brought.

Had I exercised different choices, then my life would have been different. Yet, a part of me hankered after one common aspect from those roads not taken—a master's degree—and I pondered. *Does God grant second chances?*

Presenting Outstanding Faculty Member Award
at MSM graduation ceremony

In 1991, unsolicited, my employers offered me a scholarship to read for a master's degree. I seized that opportunity. In 1993, I graduated—with excellence—with a master of science degree in management.

A STILL, SMALL VOICE

In 1997, a voice spoke directly to me: *Lorna, review the last board note you submitted for approval as soon as possible.*

The voice interrupted the morning meditation program I listened to on my car radio. I depended on this to calm my mind and prepare me for my busy schedule and hectic days as a manager of general services at the Central Bank of Trinidad and Tobago. I turned the radio up to silence the voice and resumed my meditation.

The voice was insistent—*Lorna, review the document. Lorna, review the document . . .* —and continued as though stuck on auto-repeat.

Arrival at my office did not silence the voice. I acquiesced and retrieved the month-old document and gave it a cursory look, determined to spend little time on a futile activity.

As I browsed through the document, my heart skipped a beat and then raced. I became flushed and flustered on my discovery that the document seemed convoluted. I paused, prayed, then sought a way out of my predicament, where there seemed no way.

I had invested significant time in researching and analyzing the options, shortlisted the most viable ones, and justified my recommendations to ensure a well-informed decision.

Again, the voice spoke. *Lorna, reread the document. Slowly this time.*

Scared into submission, I reviewed each line of the document and my calculations. Everything was correct. The presentation, logical. I sighed in relief, put the document away, and turned to my routine, which by now screamed for my attention.

Lorna Deane at a meeting in the board room

After two hours, I received an invitation to the board room. The board was in session, and the governor required me to present and defend my note— and be ready to answer any questions that might arise.

The following day, my note was returned, endorsed as "Approved by the Board."

DODGING DISASTER: A SAPLING'S MIRACLE

It was 8:30 one evening in 2009 when I left the bank in Toronto, Canada. Dusk had not yet fallen. I strolled toward my pine-green Volkswagen Jetta. A quick glance reassured me that everything was all right.

A mature woman stood at the intersection. She waved, then headed toward me. "Hello. Do you own this car?" she asked.

"Yes," I replied.

She said, "From the accident that happened two weeks ago, I've been watching. I wanted to see who owned this car."

"An accident?" I queried.

My mind relived the shock I experienced two weeks ago, when I saw the vehicle in the space where I had parked, completely covered with white foam.

I searched for answers: *Was this a targeted incident? What prompted it? What should I do?*

My attempts to clean the car had failed miserably. I drove to the nearest car wash with minimal visibility.

The woman spoke with urgency, as though she harbored a mystery known to her alone. "There was an accident at the corner. One car got hit, spun around, and headed directly toward your vehicle. An impact seemed certain. What happened next, I cannot understand. Do you see this small tree before your car?"

"Yes," I answered, noticing a maple sapling with a trunk diameter of four inches.

Gesticulating, she exclaimed, "That tree stopped the car. I thought, 'God must love the owner of that Jetta.' I have kept watch ever since, just to identify that person."

I inquired about the white substance.

She said, "The car burst into flames. The fire truck came and sprayed the fire out. They sprayed your car to protect it. I'm glad I met you."

She left. Her steps seemed lighter.

I examined the tree, saw the point of impact, and noticed the scorched ground beneath.

LORNA DEANE

Lorna Deane grew up on a farm in Jamaica and attended high school in Mandeville, Jamaica, where her love for literature and writing awakened as she fell in love with the power of words. She pursued undergraduate studies in English and economics at the University of Manitoba, Winnipeg, Canada, and later continued postgraduate studies at Hult International Business School, formerly the Arthur D. Little School of Management, in Boston, Massachusetts.

Her working career was in banking and finance in Jamaica, Trinidad and Tobago, and Canada.

Lorna nurtured her desire to write by joining two online communities and studying with one of Trinidad's well-known authors. Teachings from her Christian upbringing show up in many of Lorna's stories, as do influences from family relationships and dynamics.

Lorna has two sons and two grandchildren. She loves to write, garden, read, and travel.

A Lifelong Love Affair

Terry Deer

"FAIRIES, SKIP HENCE"[3]

My first fancy dress was sleeveless, with a white bodice and a lacy skirt held aloft by stiff petticoats of starchy tulle. I was to wear the dress as one of Titania's attendants in a school production of *A Midsummer Night's Dream*. It thrilled me to be onstage in something so frilly and feminine that I felt like the star instead of what I truly was, a decorative backdrop to the action.

Our teachers rewrote the play for a group of primary students, cutting it until the Bard would not have recognized his work, but that meant nothing to me. I had no lines. My big moment happened when, with two other eight-year-olds, I danced around the fairy queen as she lay sleeping before we all scampered off. Our names owed nothing to Shakespeare. We were Glitter, Blossom, and Snowdrop, and we dressed accordingly. To fit me for my role as Glitter, Mum tacked a length of tinsel to my skirt and used the leftover garland to fashion a circlet for my hair. I was resplendent.

My first school performance was at age seven, when I learned the joy and freedom of putting on a costume and pretending to be someone else. No longer Terry Deer, a shy child

---

[3] William Shakespeare, *A Midsummer Night's Dream*.

45

in a foreign country, I became Red Riding Hood. It gave me a thirst for the stage that I've never lost. I had no fear of the audience. I wanted to show off for my parents and sister, the people I loved best.

Though my first meeting with Shakespeare didn't end the way I expected, his name would henceforth carry enchantment. He gave me magic and the keen anticipation of opening night, when I would wear *the dress*. Then, alas, came crushing disappointment: a sore throat, fever, and runny nose.

Measles.

"OUR REVELS NOW ARE ENDED"[4]

"Let me not to the marriage of true minds admit impediments . . ."[5]

I stood in the living room of our home and declaimed the rich lines of Sonnet 116 to a select audience of two, my parents.

My fellow actress was my sister, Linda. She directed our scenes and designed the program, tapping out two copies on Mum's venerable typewriter. I learned lines and gathered a stack of caps, scarves, and sashes for our offstage costume changes.

As I completed my introduction and withdrew, Linda introduced the first scene, a charged encounter from *A Midsummer Night's Dream*. No longer one of the fairies, I now played Helena, the lovelorn "painted maypole."[6] Linda, who though seven years older was shorter than I, chased me around the living room until we sprinted offstage to enthusiastic applause from our generous onlookers.

---

[4] Shakespeare. *The Tempest*.
[5] Shakespeare. Sonnet 116.
[6] Shakespeare. *A Midsummer Night's Dream*.

When we were younger, Linda and I presented puppet shows, crouched behind a sheet stretched between two chairs. Our cast included bespectacled Bunny Rabbit, from the television series *Captain Kangaroo*, and an owl Linda made from a brown washcloth. I still have both, worn touchstones of my childhood.

With Linda away at college, our productions became rare and more difficult. This was our most ambitious, embracing comedy and tragedy. It required planning and rehearsal. Shakespeare's lines weren't easy for an eighth grader, but I loved the words as much as I loved sharing the stage with my sister.

Our night ended in triumph. Linda spoke the epilogue: "If we spirits have offended, think but this, and all is mended."[7] It was our final performance together. Perhaps that's why I remember it so clearly.

I'm the only one still here to remember.

"We are such stuff as dreams are made on, and our little life is rounded with a sleep."[8]

"NOT IN OUR STARS, BUT IN OURSELVES"[9]

The William and Mary theater department produced two Shakespeare plays while I was a student. I appeared in neither.

Twelfth Night was the opening show in my freshman year. I could have auditioned, but I was intimidated by the upperclassmen. It wouldn't have mattered either way, because I attended the same four years as Glennie Wade.

She's Glenn Close now, but back then she was married to Cabot Wade, whom she met while performing with *Up with People*. The tour gave her several years' head start on her fellow

---

[7] Shakespeare. *A Midsummer Night's Dream*.
[8] Shakespeare. *The Tempest*.
[9] Shakespeare. *Julius Caesar*.

students. She could act, sing, and even dance—a triple threat. By the time junior year rolled around, Glennie had taken the lead in *everything*. What, me bitter? Maybe a little, though it was hard to resent her success. She was too good. The world has since acknowledged her talent, but we saw it firsthand. Competing for roles against her brought me face to face with my limitations, a painful reality check.

In *Trojan Women*, Glennie was cast as Hecuba. It was the only time we were onstage together. I was among the nameless women mourning the loss of Troy. We wore shapeless robes of heavy burlap mesh, tennis shoes dyed black, full-face masks, and hip-length trailing veils, all to suggest a Greek chorus of Euripides' time. The veils exasperated us. I inevitably sat on mine, which tugged the mask awry. With the rest, I made my entrance, settled in my place, pulled my robe down to hide the giveaway soles of my shoes, yanked my mask into place, and wailed, "Women of Troy!" The art of coarse acting at its finest.

Glennie went on to the recognition I thought I wanted while I became a librarian and a well-regarded storyteller. I wonder which of us is happier.

"MY NAME BE BURIED WHERE MY BODY IS"[10]

How would it feel to have written the greatest works in the English language, knowing your name will never be associated with your words?

In loving the plays, I thought little about the writer Shakespeare. Why would I? The known story of the man from Stratford inspired no interest. The yawning gulf between the immortal works and the orthodox account was too wide to bridge, unless by imaginative biographers who inflated a

---

[10] Shakespeare. Sonnet 72.

handful of facts into a colorful bouquet of hot-air balloons. I couldn't care about the bland Stratford merchant. It was enough to have the words, or so I believed.

In 1984, I read *The Mysterious William Shakespeare* by Charlton Ogburn Jr., a massive book built on work begun in the 1920s by an English school teacher. J. Thomas Looney was bothered by the dissonance he perceived between the plays and their alleged author. Judging "Shake-speare" to be a pseudonym, Looney analyzed the works to uncloak a hidden writer. He believed he had found his man in Edward de Vere, seventeenth Earl of Oxford, an Elizabethan poet-courtier all but obliterated by history.

Ogburn's book taught me to care. It demolished the absurdity that the supreme English writer revealed nothing of himself in his works. Having learned how threadbare the argument for the traditional author truly is, I look to the plays to find, as Looney did, the many convincing correspondences between Oxford's life and Shakespeare's words.

Without a *smoking quill*, the authorship debate persists. Oxford might not be Shakespeare, yet the solid presence of a real person behind the name gives life to the poetry. Like Ogburn, Looney, and others, I've come to cherish that fallible, brilliant human being. I'd like him to receive the honor his works have earned.

On the other hand, it is an enthralling mystery.

"I'LL NOTE YOU IN MY BOOK OF MEMORY"[11]

I treasure Shakespeare not only for his incomparable words, his unforgettable characters, and the mystery of his identity, but also for the moments.

---

[11] Shakespeare. *Henry VI.*

In 1961, I watched Vanessa Redgrave—only twenty-four and at five feet, eleven inches, the world's tallest Rosalind—shriek with unscripted laughter because she stepped on the hem of Celia's dress in the middle of a performance of *As You Like It.*

In 1974, the student costume designer for *The House of Bernarda Alba* was up to her elbows in a vat of black dye, repurposing costumes for a cast of women in mourning. Asked what she was doing, she hilariously replied with a line adapted from *Antony and Cleopatra*: "I am dyeing Egypt."

At a Star Trek convention in 1989, I listened as Sir Patrick Stewart talked of the shenanigans so-called serious actors get up to. Far from presenting Shakespearean acting as somehow more rarified than mere television work, Sir Patrick described such hijinks as being pranked onstage with a live goldfish slipped into a goblet he had to drink from.

I will forever love the anonymous young woman seated behind me who, for Mel Gibson's sake, sat through the entirety of *Hamlet* and exclaimed in the final act, "He's not going to *die*, is he?"

In 1995, I attended Kenneth Branagh's *Othello* with a crowd of Bethune-Cookman students. Mesmerized by Laurence Fishburne's masterful performance, they shouted warnings and encouragement during a critical moment: "Don't listen to him. He's lying to you!" "She loves you, man!"

I've read that Shakespeare has been dropped from many universities' literature programs: too demanding, too irrelevant, too "dead white guy." Tell that to the Bethune-Cookman students. Dead for four centuries, the Bard still speaks to our hearts and minds, still enriches our lives. Thank you, William Shakespeare, whoever you were.

TERRY DEER

Terry Deer is a retired librarian and teacher who began life in Spokane, Washington. She has lived in nine of the contiguous states and one foreign country on her way to her current home in Tidewater, Virginia. She has been a writer since before she was ten and wrote fan fiction before it was cool. She's currently working on both a memoir of the years her family lived in England and a full-length fantasy novel. Terry has published a story in the anthology *Turning Points* and an article on the Folger Library in *The Shakespeare Oxford Newsletter*.

Besides words, Terry's passions include storytelling, the Shakespeare authorship question, cats, handwork, and jigsaw puzzles (alert readers may find at least one problem implied in that list). She currently lives in Williamsburg, Virginia, with her partner and an undisclosed number of feline companions.

Reflections on Life and Nature
Kit Dwyer

NO "I" IN RITUAL

From the living room floor, eyes open after meditation, my body stretches head to toe. Daylight spills over the horizon and penetrates the wall of windows. Once-hidden hues, mostly green, show gold and orange tinges of summer's wane.

A tiny hummingbird visits each flowerpot on the deck, then rests for a moment on the railing. Its green iridescent belly glows. A yellow-bellied sapsucker finishes a turn at the feeder before it flitters safely to the forest with a prize.

A gentle rain begins to fall under almost imperceptible thunder. Sudden sunbeams strike out from dark globs of pewter clouds onto still-dripping trees. Imagine a rainbow somewhere. Good fortune noted.

Adjust today's intention list on the kitchen counter: *Write thank-you notes. Walk later.*

Tear out the square of Earl Grey. Sniff the fine mesh, then drop it into the hot mug like a lure on a fishing line. Read the saying on the tag. Down the three capsules on the counter with a sip from the top.

Collect the mug, the phone, the book, the list, and rise the steps to my writing space, careful to include a smile and not add more drips on the carpet.

DEATH IMPRESSIONS

The coffin harbors
White satin pleats
Ambient stillness
A face
Closed eyelids glued cold
Expression excluded
Worn-out shell
People whispering
Loss whimpering

—

An old woman I didn't know well
My dogs
Then, my sister
My brother-in-law
Parents
Friends
It never ends

—

Like leaves and petals go to ground
Some slowly
Some stormily
The dead fall
To places beyond
Needs erased
Towering trees stand watch
Longer than we can stay

Kit Dwyer

JOSIE'S GIFT

Plastic grapes in the hallway, plastic wrap on the divan,
my visit to Grandma's house began.
Fur coats and mothballs behind the door,
quiet and dark, it always smelled poor.
Soft, wrinkly hands bid my younger self explore
one gift from her jewelry box to have forevermore.
A set of blue enamel, pink roses, with rhines,
the kind with brass earlobe screws, could be mine.
From behind me, she held them against my white locks
as I sat before the oval mirror—for dress-up mock.
A cookie from her kitchen and her warm hug—
there used to be two, before move-aways tugged.
Now only one, in all its splendor.
Love endures, more than grandeur.

Grandma
Josie's
earring

STRIDES THROUGH DIVORCE

I could have listened, but I didn't hear.
I could have tried more, but I was afraid.
I could have struggled on, but I was intimidated.
I could have laughed, but I cried.
I could have stayed silent, but I spoke up.
I could have lied, but I knew better.
I could have accused, but I pardoned.
I could have stayed the same, but I ventured.
I could have given up, but I was determined.
I could have looked away.
But instead, I looked up.

SEEKING SOUL

Longing, I step outside to discover the nature of the day.

Hot mug and cold air blur my vision. Resign to other senses.

Perhaps it is in the cries of alluring loons, bickering blue jays, tittering titmouse, chattering chickadee, and whapping woodpecker.

Perhaps it is in the nuthatch's taut flits to grab a bug or cautious sip from the tree trunk hole.

Perhaps it is in the breeze between the outstretched tips of eagle wings, circling.

Perhaps it is in my glimpse of the moon's change beyond branches with dark, stubborn leaves.

Perhaps it was in our shared eye-spark when we greeted each other.

Perhaps it was when I stroked your soft fur and kept our ritual of play, walk, eat.

Perhaps it was in the places where your tongue brushed my skin, or you leaned against my leg.

Perhaps it is in the clatter at the shore where waves talk like people splashing on rocks.

Perhaps it is under the surface where your paws paddled, while you sniffed over fish and turtles and otter, seeking your yellow ball now out of sight.

Perhaps it is in the moment I find your soul, nestled under my rib, and heed your fervent lessons: Care for those who need care. Keep seeking.

DECIDING

"Mom, look! That bird is taking a seed right out of Dad's hand."

"I don't think he'd mind if you joined him out there."

"Sorry, Dad, I didn't mean to ruin it with the sound of the door."

"That's okay. Come sit next to me, then be very still. I think it will come back."

"Why would that bird take a seed from your hand? How did you get it to do that?"

"Well, the black-capped chickadee's the most likely of the birds at our feeder to be so bold. Remember that book you gave me for my birthday? It says that chickadees are extremely curious. So, I tried holding out my palm with a few of their favorite black sunflower seeds. I had to be quite still and become part of the scene."

Dad kept his hand laid against the railing with his offering while he said to the chickadee, "Shik-a-dee-dee-dee-dee."

"Shik-a-dee-dee-dee-dee," I mimicked back. "Maybe that makes us friend-birds, only bigger."

"Oh, here it comes again! I think he likes you."

"Is it a he-bird? How can you tell? I like the way this one tips its head from side to side before he hops toward you. He's deciding, each time he comes back from the forest, isn't he?"

"That's a way for this small one to stay safe. It checks out for danger, like when you're at the top of the hill holding your sled, deciding which route to descend and when it's clear to shove off."

"Boy, oh boy, I can hardly wait for winter to go sledding. I don't think you'll be out here holding your hand for the birds when it's cold and snowing."

"Probably not, but by then there will be new bird visitors to study."

KIT DWYER

Kit Dwyer hails from the countryside of Pennsylvania. Her passion for writing bloomed in the third grade with poetry. Her career as a project manager in the mapping industry led her to Toastmasters International, reigniting her fervor for both writing and public speaking. Upon retirement, Kit's enthusiasm for capturing personal history came to life, and she founded Firsthand Memories to help others preserve their unique stories.

Today, Kit calls southern Missouri home, where she enjoys lake life with her husband, Dave. When she's not crafting memoirs, she's embracing the great outdoors, exploring the US, bicycling, hiking, and cherishing moments with her two grandchildren. Dive deeper into Kit's world and her inspiring work at FirsthandMemories.com.

Stories from the Home Front: World War II

Lucille Ellson

D-DAY ANNIVERSARY 2024

June 6, 2024. I watched on TV the eightieth D-Day commemoration events at the American Cemetery in Normandy, France. I was overwhelmed with sadness as I viewed the 9,400 white crosses, each of which honored an American World War II hero. In the front row of the ten thousand attendees, hunched down in their wheelchairs, clutching their canes, sat a few surviving veterans. White-haired, no smiles on their wrinkled faces, and some teary-eyed—told me they were remembering painful wartime experiences. Tears dribbled down my cheeks, too, as I was reminded

Floyd in his dress whites

Floyd and his company

59

of anxious days I spent when Floyd was a US Navy officer aboard a supply ship.

After viewing the D-Day commemorative events, I know the battles and heroes of WWII are well documented in history books, movies, and pictures. But where are the stories of my own family's home front heroes preserved? Since I went back home when Floyd was at sea, I have home front stories of Swan Lake Farm to tell.

WORLD WAR II TELEGRAM

By the 1944 Christmas season, Mom and Dad Beneke had welcomed six family members, including me, to make Swan Lake Farmhouse their home during World War II. Floyd, now on duty aboard the USS *Windrush* as the navy officer, was comforted knowing I'd be well cared for awaiting the birth of our first child, Jane Lee.

During the school vacation, my high school friend Marcia Thompson, now a teacher, had planned a baby shower for me—a fun event several other classmates would attend.

The Benekes, with Lucille in the back row, second from right

Lucille Ellson

Marcia was married but continued teaching in Iowa; her husband was drafted and in the army in Germany.

Shortly after Christmas, the date for the highly anticipated shower arrived. A sunny day with the ground covered with a blanket of newly fallen snow made a perfect day for my exciting adventure of a baby shower.

Midmorning, the telephone rang, and my mother answered. Her voice and composure told me something—not good—had happened. She finally got the words out of her mouth. Marcia received the dreaded WWII telegram: Her husband had been killed in action.

The shower was canceled. Mom, Dad, and I immediately went to their home to be with them. Later, my mother's friend, Cecelia Ford, came over with a much-appreciated shower gift, a white batiste baby dress. Clothing and fabrics were impossible to buy during the war. The dress was given to the Ford's baby boy, but the husband declared, "No dress on my boy."

Jane wore the dress for her first picture and her baptism.

After the first semester, Marcia resigned her teaching job and joined the WACs overseas, where she met and married Army Chaplain Bill Hogeville. After the war, they lived in Hagerstown, Maryland, where Bill was pastor of a Christian church for many years.

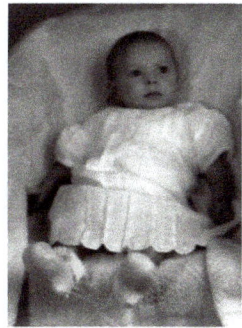

Two-month-old Jane

ROAD TRIP SURPRISE

In June 1945, Floyd was given a two-week furlough before he boarded an oil tanker bound for an eight-month trip to Iran. Floyd was excited to spend time with baby Jane, now almost five months old.

Floyd, Lucille, and Jane, 1945

My sister Marjorie's birthday was June 15, and my dad thought it would be fun to surprise her with a visit from Lt. Floyd and baby Jane. With gas rationed and tires off the market, a seventy-five-mile road trip to George, Iowa, was a luxury.

The morning of the trip, the baby basket full of Jane's needs, a flat of strawberries, and a birthday cake were loaded into the trunk. After an hour of driving on a dusty gravel road, the car began to swerve. Floyd pulled over onto the shoulder and announced a flat tire. The trunk had to be unloaded to get to the spare tire. When the car stopped, Jane awoke and started crying. Lt. Floyd was unhappy changing the tire in his dress white uniform. But before long, we were all happy travelers again.

Marjorie's husband, Perry Jensen, a veterinarian, had been rejected by the draft. He served by caring for farm animals during the war. The Jensens lived in the apartment above the office. Upon arriving, Dad knocked on the door, expecting to be greeted by a surprised Marjorie. Several knocks produced no answer. Checking in at the office, Dad got a real surprise: The secretary informed him the Jensens were staying with friends, Geert and George Summa, while their newly varnished floors dried. We got directions to the Summas' home.

Floyd knocked, and when the door opened, Marjorie was as surprised as Dad had hoped she would be. The Summas graciously invited us to spend the day—a fun day of surprises for all.

LUCILLE ELLSON

Lucille Ellson grew up on a family farm near Laurens, Iowa, with two sisters and four brothers. She rode to school in a horse-drawn bus for her first two years.

After graduating from the University of Northern Iowa, which was then called Iowa State Teachers College, Lucille's teaching career included eight years in Iowa public schools and fourteen at the Iowa Braille and Sight Saving School in Vinton, Iowa.

Lucille and her husband Floyd co-authored his memoir, *My First Hundred Years*, in 2016. Her memoir, *My Last Hundred Years and Change*, was written by Lucille and her son Jim and published in 2023. Floyd and Lucille were both centenarians when they wrote their life stories.

Lucille lives in Orlando, where she and Floyd moved after their retirement. After sixty-nine years of marriage, Floyd passed away in 2012.

Animal Encounters

Judy Fink

HECTOR

I remember one very dry, hot Pennsylvania summer; I walked outside to my backyard deck and heard a panicked cry. There, lying on the floor, was a newborn baby robin crying for its mother, its eyes not open, only fuzz covering its tiny wings and body. I realized the mother could not carry the baby back up to the nest, so I gently placed it in an empty shoebox with a soft washcloth inside. I phoned the Pittsburgh Aviary for advice and explained about the chick.

The gentleman said, "Sometimes in drought years, a mother bird can't feed more than one baby, so she'll push the weaker one out of the nest. You realize the Aviary can't take it."

"I don't want you to take it. I just want to know how to help it," I answered.

"Feed it bits of canned cat food for protein and eyedroppers of water," he said.

I named him *Hector*.

I fed him as instructed and called my neighbor Gina to come over to see the little guy. His mouth opened so wide; it seemed bigger than his head as I fed him cat food and water.

Sadly, Hector only lived for a few days. My kids and I held a small funeral, then buried him behind our house.

Gina and her husband, Jerry, were outside. I said, "Hector died."

Jerry, his face showing sadness and deep concern, said, "I'm so sorry. Was Hector a relative of yours?"

Gina and I smiled. "No, Hector was a baby bird I tried to save."

"Baby bird? Seriously? Here I was really feeling sorry for you, thinking it was a family member or friend, certainly not a baby bird!"

Laughing, I said, "I know, but thanks for the condolences anyway."

CHIPMUNK ENCOUNTER

Behind our first home in Pennsylvania, we installed a pre-made pond at the base of our sloped backyard hillside. We added a small waterfall and bog with plants to help keep the system clean. Birds and small animals came daily to drink from the pond.

Each day, I sat on the backyard deck, enjoying the beauty and nature of the setting. One cute furry chipmunk made a daily run down the hill to get water and any fallen seeds from my two hanging bird feeders. Cautiously, he would come out into the open to gather seeds, knowing I was there, then scurry back to the underbrush.

One afternoon while eating some cheese curls, I wondered if he would eat one. I placed it on the path he usually took, then sat very still and waited. Scampering out of the plants, he headed toward the water. Spotting the cheese curl, he stopped dead, stretched out his neck, sniffed the bright orange object in his path, grabbed the curl, and ran back to safety.

I continued placing pieces but kept moving them closer to my seat. He was tentative at first, but he must have felt the risk was worth it. Slowly, he came closer every time I moved the treat. I put one on top of my shoe and sat very still. By then, he had little fear of me, so he took it and ran. Finally, I held the cheese curl in my extended hand and waited. Cautiously, he took it from my hand and comfortably sat there nibbling his reward. After eating several pieces, he stuffed the remaining curls in his cheeks for later and scurried off.

I hoped I didn't give him a bellyache, but I thoroughly enjoyed getting up close and personal with that furry little chipmunk.

BIRTHDAY WITH VICTORIA

The year was 2005, celebrating a milestone birthday: *sixty* years old.

Joe asked, "How do you want to spend your day?"

Without hesitation, I answered, "The zoo."

The Pittsburgh Zoo was established in 1898. It isn't very big compared to some zoos, but it is quaint and always improving. I remember when they added a state-of-the-art aquarium in 1967 with sharks and manta rays.

We enjoyed taking our children and later our grandchildren to the zoo on many occasions when they came to visit. On this day, the zoo was offering pictures with Victoria, a very large female elephant, for a fee of five dollars. I jumped at the chance.

Victoria was beautiful but extremely intimidating. Being that close to this behemoth animal, I noticed the coarse, long hair on her leathery skin along with long, lush eyelashes. She lowered her eyes to look into mine, and we made contact. I was somewhat afraid to touch her. I later regretted not taking that rare opportunity.

Victoria, Joe, and me

Joe wanted to feel her leathery skin, so he put his hand on her side, and she leaned into him. He said he could sense her size and strength with that slight movement.

You observe animals in zoos usually at a good distance. This close encounter was beyond special. I only wish I had touched her and made that connection a little deeper, but I still am in awe at the memory of standing so close to this beautiful creature.

GIRAFFE ENCOUNTER

Around 2019, our family, visiting from Pennsylvania, joined us to tour the Giraffe Ranch in Dade City, Florida, to experience these majestic animals up close.

We were told by our guide, "Do not try to touch or pet the giraffes. In the wild, they are *prey* animals and will bolt if they feel danger. Since the safari truck we will be riding in has a roof, if one is spooked, it could suddenly raise its enormous head, causing injury."

The guide informed us that each giraffe's spotted coat variation is as unique as a fingerprint. As we drove near the enclosure, we saw them approaching the fence, anticipating their treat. Their sheer size was overwhelming at sixteen to eighteen feet tall. Unafraid, they stretched their heads into the open sides of the truck, eagerly sticking out their twenty-inch tongues as we hand-fed them cabbage, green onions, and branches with tasty leaves.

Feeding the giraffes

Following the lead of the older giraffes, an adorable

baby, perhaps eight or nine feet tall, approached. Everyone in the truck *oohed* and *aahed* as he chomped on his offered treats.

One of the most striking things was the giraffes' big brown eyes with lush long eyelashes . . . beautiful.

If only we were allowed to stroke their massive heads or necks, what a thrill that would be! But respecting the animals and their safety was more important. Just being in their awesome presence was more than enough.

STINGRAY CITY

Grand Cayman Island, our next cruise ship stopover, offered an adventure tour to Stingray City, a shallow area where stingrays were abundant. As our small boat slowed, multiple large round black spots were seen moving under the crystal-clear water toward the vessel. It was a bit daunting. The guide said, "Don't worry. They're just like dogs. They know when it's dinnertime and come running."

Donning snorkel gear, we entered the shoulder-high water and were instructed how to feed these unique creatures, squid being their favorite. The stingrays' mouths are under their bodies, eyes on top. The staff gave us small pieces of squid and instructed us to wedge a piece between two fingers while keeping our palms up and flat. The rays, in turn, glided over our hands and sucked the squid into their mouths. Each smooth white underbelly felt like silk as they glided over our hands, accepting the offered treats.

Stingray encounter

Moving from one person to the next, they often rubbed our legs with their satiny underside. The long *stinger* tail is their weapon when threatened, so we were instructed to be careful not to accidentally step on the rays. "Shuffle your feet through the sandy bottom to avoid this," the staff said.

One guide put his hands under one of the bigger rays and raised it to the surface so everyone could get a closer look. The top layer was completely opposite from the silky underbelly we had felt; this was dark-gray to black in color and felt like rough sandpaper. Everyone took turns gently stroking and marveling at their unique skin texture.

Very few people ever get to see and touch creatures living under the ocean's waves. I was more than thrilled to be one of them.

SLITHER

I love my Florida screened-in lanai. Joe and I sit out there for a while just about every day. Past our backyard fence is a small canal where wildlife is abundant. Snowy white egrets and blue herons wade along the water's edge in search of small fish or frogs. Predatory eagles and osprey are often seen swooping for prey. I even witnessed two alligators in a rarely seen mating encounter.

Walking onto the lanai one afternoon, movement flashed in my peripheral vision. A four-foot black snake swiftly slithered across the pavers and ended up coiled in the far corner of our screened-in birdcage.

I screamed, "Joe, there's a *snake* on the lanai!"

He came, and we tried to figure out how to safely remove the reptile for release. Joe, my resident small game hunter, got out his professional gear—a large black trash can and a long-handled Swiffer Duster. He laid the can on its side and urged the snake to enter.

That snake wanted nothing to do with it. Repeatedly, it lunged toward Joe, mouth wide open, threatening to bite, trying to protect itself.

Finally, Joe coaxed it in and took it outside, dumping the snake into nearby shrubbery. We tried to locate how it got inside but couldn't see any openings.

I went indoors but soon stepped back outside. I couldn't believe it; the snake was *back*, coiled in the same corner!

"Joe, the snake's back!" I yelled.

Joe, now an expert, caught it again and dumped it farther from the house. We got on hands and knees searching for its entrance. Finally, we found a small, shredded patch of screen, which Joe sealed with a sturdy metal plate. I hope that reptile finally realizes he is not welcome on my lanai—ever.

JUDY FINK

Judy Fink is a relatively new writer from the hills of Pittsburgh, Pennsylvania—Steeler Country. A lifelong desire to write entered her into the community of Life Writers through classes in The Villages, Florida, where she now resides with her husband, Joe.

When not writing or editing, Judy loves playing samba card games with neighbors and friends. That same group holds monthly book club meetings and enjoys occasional lunches together. Her micro-memoirs, "I Remember" and

"My Pink Bicycle," were published in The Poet's Corner of *The Villages Daily Sun* newspaper. Judy's goal is to create a history of her life for future generations. Each life is filled with stories, and she wants to tell hers.

Moving—Again and Again and Again

Julie Folkerts

WHERE NOW?

- Another new home.
- Another new school.
- Will they make fun of my overbite?
- Will I be accepted?
- Will making friends be easy this time?
- Will we have friendly neighbors, or will they keep to themselves?
- Will the house, apartment, or trailer be furnished?
- If not, do they have a used furniture store?
- Will I need to share a bed with my younger sister, or will we sleep on aluminum folding cots in our sleeping bags?
- Will we walk or ride a bus to school?
- Will other United States Geological Survey, Topographic Division, families relocate here?

My younger sister and me

73

- Will a Lutheran church exist, or will we attend another Christian denomination?
- Will I need allergy shots? A new location means new allergens: house dust, mold, mildew, grass, weeds, and trees.
- The climate will be different.
- How long will we live here?

Statistics show effects on young children who move frequently include . . .

- Evoking emotions, including sadness, anxiety, excitement, and a sense of loss. Leaving behind familiar surroundings, friends, and routines can contribute to these emotional responses.
- Frequent moves disrupt kids' friendships and are most problematic for introverted, anxious, and inflexible kids.
- Stress due to repeated transitions can undermine a child's sense of control over their life.
- Moving is stressful for kids, leaving behind friends, teachers, and comforts they have grown accustomed to. They have no say in where they're going or what they are leaving behind.
- Research shows that moving during middle school is probably the worst age for changing schools.
- Researchers tell us that everyone needs time to adjust—often as long as sixteen months. The most stressful time is two weeks before and two weeks after the move.

Fortunately for me, my parents took moving in stride—it was time to pack up again.

MOVE NUMBER THIRTY-FOUR

Spearfish, South Dakota

I knew little about Spearfish except that Mom's best friend, Delores (whose husband also worked for the USGS), grew up there. Delores shared how beautiful it was in the summer months and that it is a tourist stop between Mount Rushmore and Devil's Tower.

It was the summer before my sophomore year of high school. I was sixteen and excited about getting my learner's permit. My parents suggested I find a summer job to keep busy. Working as a motel maid in a busy tourist spot was not my ideal job, but it would have to do. It was a small, twelve-unit motel on the edge of town just off the main highway in the direction of the Spearfish Canyon Scenic Byway connecting the city of Lead. This route has an unparalleled view of the landscape sprinkled with waterfalls, flora, and wildlife.

I worked seven days a week—no days off. I rode my ten-speed bike about a mile to begin work at 6:00 a.m. Another girl, Sarah, and I worked as a team. We switched chores daily—one took the bathrooms, and the other handled the beds and living area. There is no need to tell you which part I was least fond of.

My other summer pastime found me at the local swimming pool. I became great friends with the pool manager, Gary. He was in his late twenties and married. We enjoyed flirting with each other. As a budding photographer, he asked me to model for him—posing at the pool and in a field full of sunflowers. That greatly

Julie modeling at pool

affected my self-esteem, as I was a little short on that. Later, he told me he submitted the photos to *Seventeen* magazine. I never heard if they were liked.

MOVE NUMBER FORTY-THREE
Culbertson, Montana (Part One)

This work assignment for Dad began with an endless drive—799 miles from Denver, sixty miles from the Canadian border, and twenty-three miles west of the North Dakota state line. The town was small, with only about 700 citizens and the Missouri River winding nearby.

To try to meet people, my sister and I drove my parents' large gray Imperial up and down the short main street. We received many fascinating looks. Always inquisitive about new girls in town, guys motioned for us to stop in a nearby grocery store parking lot. It felt safe enough, and fortunately, it was.

On our first outing, we met Randy and Bob riding in a shiny blue-and-white Mustang. Bob was friendly, but Randy caught my eye immediately. Brown hair, blue eyes, gorgeous straight white teeth, about five feet eleven, with a fun spirit. We chatted for about an hour and then invited them to our rental house to continue our conversation. I knew Dad would appreciate having us close by.

The evening ended with a spring in my step and glassy eyes—I felt an immediate attraction to Randy. Each day after work, Randy came by and began to show me around Culbertson, introducing me to his friends. He invited me to his family's ranch west of town for dinner to meet his younger brothers and parents. I felt he was as intrigued with me as I was with him. We were both twenty—the summer of 1978.

One summer day, when Randy was at work, washing the outside windows of a mustard seed mill where he worked, the forklift basket broke, plunging him thirty-five feet to the ground, landing on his face. He was life-flighted to Billings for traumatic care.

MOVE NUMBER FORTY-THREE
Culbertson, Montana (Part Two)

Randy's best friend, Bob, came to deliver the news about Randy, and I lost it. He hugged me as we sat on the cold cement steps. In shock, all that came out of my mouth were questions. "Does Billings have a trauma hospital? Are his parents with him? Will he be okay?"

Bob's answers to these questions drove me deeper into despair.

My crying became sobbing and heaving.

Bob said, "From what Randy's mom shared earlier, Randy broke his nose, his jaw, his cheeks. Most of his teeth were chipped or gone, and the eggshell-type bones behind his eyes were shattered. Surgeons can't begin surgery until the swelling has subsided." Bob said he would let me know if he heard anything further.

Barely able to walk back into the house, I found Mom waiting for me. We hugged as I recounted Bob's news. I then staggered to my tiny room, crawled into my sleeping bag on the aluminum cot, buried my face in my pillow, and bawled for what seemed like hours.

How could this horrible accident occur to someone so special? How long would Randy be in Billings? I knew it was only about six more weeks before we would be moving back south again. Dad's assignment was a short one.

The following day, after work, Bob appeared at the door to ask if I would like to go to Billings with him to see Randy. Of course, I would, but I was scared. What would Randy look like? Could I keep it together?

Billings was three hundred miles away—a six-hour drive. We started the following morning and would stay with Bob's friends or in hotel rooms with Randy's family.

MOVE NUMBER FORTY-THREE
Culbertson, Montana (Part Three)

Arriving in Billings after the long drive from Culbertson, and at speeds I had never traveled, Bob pulled into the motel where Randy's family was staying. When we entered the room, they jumped up to hug and welcome us. Looking around, I noticed how cluttered and crowded it was. I questioned whether I could fit in the small space with everyone else.

The family had recently returned from the hospital, where they had sat with Randy and questioned the doctors as they made their rounds. When asked how Randy was, his mother responded, "As good as can be expected at this time."

What does that mean? I have no idea. Is he conscious? In a coma? Can he talk? I was afraid to ask too many questions, so I let it go. *I will see for myself tomorrow.*

Bob and Randy had friends who now lived in Billings, so Bob suggested we stop by and see them. I went along with whatever Bob wanted—he was driving. Arriving at his friend Sandy's house, I was introduced. Sitting in their living room, Sandy's boyfriend grabbed a large glass water pipe, which they called a bong.

What is that for? I quickly learned it was to smoke pot.

Within minutes of passing the pipe around, they politely asked if I'd like a smoke. I tried to be graceful when saying

NO. I didn't do drugs—I never did—and I didn't plan on starting. So, for the rest of the evening, I sat and listened to their memories about Randy while inhaling secondhand marijuana smoke.

Arriving at Randy's room the next day, following Bob, I stopped suddenly, afraid to enter. *Take a deep breath. Be strong. Don't cry.*

I stepped into the room.

MOVE NUMBER FORTY-THREE

Culbertson, Montana (Conclusion)

My eyes immediately focused on the tubes, cords, and monitors hooked to Randy. His head and face were severely swollen, with his forehead three times its normal size. His jaw was wired shut. His eyes were sunken, black-and-blue sockets, and his head bandaged up, much like a mummy.

Fight with all you have. Grab Bob's arm. Don't collapse.

With Randy's family present, I was at a loss for what to say, but I managed to whisper, "Praying for you." Not knowing if Randy knew we were there, Bob and I left after a few minutes. We would return tomorrow for another go-round.

Randy before the accident

Recovery would be a long road with many surgeries ahead. The doctor asked for a recent picture to give to the plastic surgeon. I volunteered one of the only pictures I had of Randy—I didn't want to part with it, but I understood the need.

∞

Preparing to leave Culbertson next week, we invited friends we'd made over the summer for a going-away party. Unknown to me, Randy had returned from Billings. Accompanied by his brothers, Randy walked into the backyard. I had to take a second look before I realized it was him. Randy asked if he could speak to me alone and grabbed my hand as we walked to the front of the house. He said, "I wanted you to know that if this accident hadn't happened, I was going to ask you to marry me. Now, so much has changed. It wouldn't be right to ask now."

I was speechless. *How should I respond? What can I say that is compassionate?* I dug deep inside and said, "Don't worry about that now. You need to finish your surgeries and continue healing." We hugged, and I whispered, "I'll continue to pray for you."

JULIE FOLKERTS

Julie Folkerts recently became a first-time grandmother. She is a breast cancer survivor and a retired legal assistant with a bachelor of business administration degree. Over her twenty-five-year career, she worked for law firms in Denver, Dallas, and Houston.

She was born in Denver, Colorado, but at the age of one, Julie's family began moving two to three times per year for her father's career as a cartographer for the United States

Geological Survey. She is currently writing her memoir about the places and people she and her family encountered in their more than forty-five moves. In addition, she writes a blog at www.Goodbye-Girl.com.

Julie enjoys crafting, quilting, and scrapbooking, as well as reading and writing. She lives with her husband in Katy, Texas.

Love Notes

Barbara Anne Gardner, EdD

MY TREASURE

A journal entry three months after my eighty-nine-year-old mother moved in with me and my cats in Brooklyn, New York:

What a beautiful morning. Mom is here with me and Iwe (ee-way) and Wena (when-uh), my little tabby cats from Zimbabwe. It's still and tranquil. The sun-filled kitchen opens into the dining room. The gentlest of breezes whispers over us from open windows, and the bright autumn light shines on the sleeping, sweet-tempered Iwe. His long body is draped across the dining room windowsill. His little sister, Wena, sleeps curled in a soft fur ball on a chair near her brother's perch. Mom sits at the kitchen table engrossed in her favorite pastime, her head capped by a soft crown of white hair, slightly bent over the book she's reading. I sit across from her with a view of all three as I write.

Mom and me

83

I wish this instant would stretch forever. To have my beloveds peacefully coexisting around me. Each entity doing its own thing. Unbidden, tears fill my eyes as I know they will not be here with me forever. Perfection would be to fully enjoy this moment without fear's muffled drumbeat playing in the back of my mind. I must imprint this memory on my heart.

Mom being here has been the best gift I could ever have. To get to know her all over again, and to see the pattern of her life as she gracefully ages. To see how she organizes herself to face each day and deal with whatever it brings. Observing and interacting with her has made me more grateful and understanding.

As I told her one morning last week when we hugged, "You are my treasure."

She responded, her voice cracking with emotion, "And you are mine."

NANNY'S GARDEN

Nanny and me

Having traveled by bus, train, and taxi, I was finally home. The long trip between Amherst, Massachusetts, where I was enrolled as a doctoral student, to our family's apartment in Brooklyn, New York, was finally over.

I dropped my bag, shed my coat, and hugged each family member. My adored and adoring Nanny invited me to take a tour of her garden. Bespectacled and soft-spoken,

Nanny was my maternal grandmother, the anchor I was fortunate enough to have grown up with along with my parents and little brother.

All tiredness disappeared as soon as I entered her large, sun-filled room. Bright, almost blinding sunlight bathed all manner of greenery mixed with red and yellow plants in green and terra cotta pots that covered the long windowsill. Dark-green, tiger-striped snake plants, trimmed in yellow, pointed vigorously to heaven. Shiny, green of a slightly lighter shade, heart-shaped philodendrons gracefully spilled out of their pots. The oval, smooth-edged, and leathery yellow-and-red of the crotons provided contrasting colors among the greens.

More green plants—and their cuttings sprouting in water—lived in a variety of clear glass jars and bottles on the top of the dark brown chest of drawers that stood in front of the window. The cuttings were what I called the "plant babies." Still more plants were clustered in pots on the floor on the right side of the chest. Nanny and I slowly inspected and marveled at each plant. I loved this ritual.

The scene was of a happy community of plants and plant cuttings keeping each other company. They were tended with care and love by Nanny's always busy, soft, and gently gnarled hands. Her calm, patient, and loving spirit was expressed in her calm, patient, and loving tending of this cherished garden.

AFRICAN MEMORIES
Senegal (November 1976)

First sight of the African continent.
Early morning, fly over inky green trees.
Atlantic Ocean's white foam laps the Senegalese coast.
En route to Peace Corps volunteer post in Liberia.

Liberia (1976–1978)

Too excited to sleep.

"Learn to take time."

Zorzor, home of the Rural Teacher Training Institute, across the road from traditional Loma village, Fissibu.

Mandingos and Lebanese, two tribes of immigrant traders and shopkeepers.

Niger (1983)

The JFK Bridge spans the River Niger.

Camels lope through streets behind cars and cross the bridge with them, too.

Stately desert nomads glide through town.

Dust and sand everywhere . . .

Zimbabwe (1995–1997)

The *kopje* (co-pea), the highest point to view Harare, the beautiful capital city.

Purple jacaranda trees form gentle canopies across wide boulevards.

World epicenter of HIV/AIDS lacks enough caskets to bury the dead.

Two lovebirds snuggle on a branch in the euphorbia tree.

Eritrea (1997)

After decades of civil war, one of the world's highest rates of amputees.

Asmara's graceful date palms stir in the breeze.

In the cool evening, large families walk peacefully, many abreast, down wide streets.

Muezzin calls the Islamic faithful to prayer. Minutes later, bells ring out from the Coptic Church.

Ghana (1998–2001)

Horrific slave forts on the Atlantic coast.

Akosombo Dam, hydroelectric power.

Ylang ylang in bloom outside my window.

Enstoolment as a queen mother in an Ashanti town. The same people sold my ancestors into slavery.

Namibia (2004)

Sunset flight over caramel-colored Namib Desert sand dunes.

The Etosha Pan and National Park. Giraffes have eyelashes to die for!

Windhoek looks like an MGM movie set.

Graceful Herero women in their fitted bodices, long skirts, and shawls. Headresses shaped like the horns of their cattle.

A young nation creates a post-apartheid education system worthy of its precious people.

The Unforgettable EB

Two years ago, our first encounter was in the sunny lanai of my cousin's Florida home. There she was, a small-framed, elegant lady resplendent in the soft folds of a multicolored African gown. A matching scarf covered her head, stylishly anchored at the side with a soft knot. Bedecked in a necklace of white cowrie shells, a cowrie-shelled bracelet also encircled one of her small wrists. Her feet were enclosed in white sandals.

"Hi. How are you? I'm happy to meet you."

A welcoming smile graced her unlined, mocha-colored face. Eyeglasses framed her bright eyes. Her voice was strong and cheerful, and her hand grasped mine warmly. Even though we were strangers, I felt at ease. As if we'd known each other forever, we shared about our lives and families. I was grieving the recent loss of my mother after having taken care of her for three years. EB listened compassionately and offered heartfelt encouragement I deeply appreciated.

Soon after our visit, I learned EB was battling cancer for the second time. She was undergoing chemotherapy every two weeks, which left her exhausted.

I was stunned. The person I'd encountered exuded a powerful life force. EB was retired, but it was evident she hadn't retired from life. I was encouraged by her joie de vivre and her determination to "live as long as possible."

Earlier this year, I returned to Florida and met EB again. Cancer had ravaged her body, yet she remained calm and lucid. She expressed to me deep appreciation for her loving family and her Buddhist practice—just days before she peacefully passed away.

I will never forget the profound example of EB's radiant, never-give-up spirit as she faced life's ultimate challenge.

TIME TO SAY GOODBYE

During his first viewing of my African art collection, the young man walked into my living room and saw the piano.

"Wow. Do you play?"

"No, I don't. Started learning as a child but didn't continue. Actually, I'm moving, and I'll be selling it."

"Could I buy it?"

"Sure."

The widest of smiles spread across his handsome face. "I compose and perform my own music that I want to touch peoples' hearts."

Relieved and a little sad, I felt at peace knowing the piano would be well used.

I'd lived with my family—until I was sixteen and went away to college—on the third floor of this Brooklyn apartment building. My brother and I lost interest in playing the piano when we were young. It became a place to display framed family pictures and Ghanaian and Zimbabwean sculpture. Bulging family photo albums were neatly stacked atop the piano bench and on the carpeted floor between its legs. Mom, the family photographer, had com-

The young musician and the piano

piled the albums with love and care. Our piano bore witness to golden family memories, our far-flung travel experiences, and our love of African art.

When I moved back to the same building in 2001, my apartment was on the first floor. Mom moved downstairs to live with me. The piano came with her. It was given pride of place in our living room. Now, two years after her passing, I was moving to Florida and leaving so much behind. Dreading the chaos, I'd create in my home and in my heart, I'd procrastinated dismantling anything.

The piano was removed without mishap. A bittersweet feeling welled up inside me when I looked at the empty space. Time to make a choice: Focus on loss or look forward—forever grateful for golden memories, ready to make new ones.

DR. BARBARA ANNE GARDNER

Peace and peacemaking have been strong, vibrant threads Dr. Barbara Anne Gardner has woven into the fabric of her life. At age thirteen she wanted to work for the United Nations. Growing up in New York City, she enjoyed meeting people from many cultures.

Barbara Anne's assignment as a Peace Corps volunteer in Liberia and her academic training spurred her on to a twenty-five-year career as an education specialist in international development. She worked in twenty-three countries in sub-Saharan Africa and lived for nine years in five of them.

Upon returning to New York, Barbara Anne taught for nine years in a small private college founded by Puerto Ricans. The majority of her students were working single mothers who were bilingual and usually the first in their families to attend college. Their grit and determination to succeed constantly inspired her.

Barbara Anne's goal is to touch people's hearts with her memoir.

Barbara Anne Gardner, EdD

The Road Less Ridden

David Godin

WHY PAY MORE?

Naturally, it happened in the evening, not during the day when repair shops were open, and on Sunday, when businesses closed early.

Lisa and I were in Virginia on our first long-distance ride and needed gas. After filling up, Lisa noticed her back tire was flat. Not the front tire, naturally, but the inaccessible back.

We filled the tire at the air pump. It immediately deflated. Lisa rolled the bike forward, and I knelt behind to look for the leak but couldn't find it. We called roadside assistance.

The sympathetic operator said, "Sorry you are experiencing trouble," and called a tow truck.

When the truck arrived, an equally sympathetic driver said, "The Harley shop ain't open till morning. I'll park your bike in my garage and meet you there about 8:00 a.m. tomorrow."

He left us at the gas station with one bike and two large hard-sided luggage bags. After figuring out the logistics, we rode off with Lisa seated behind me, holding the heavy bags like outriggers. We weren't going far, lugging all that bulky gear.

Luggage bag

A mile later, we saw an illuminated sign outside a nondescript hotel, shining in the night like the star of Bethlehem:

$35

Why pay more?

Why pay more? I'll tell you why. When we entered the room, I flipped on the light switch, and the wall-mounted 40-watt fixture struggled to illuminate the room. The bedspreads on the two queen-sized beds didn't match the room or each other, and the bathroom door wouldn't close because the top hinge had pulled out. We plugged our communicators and phones into the receptacle and went to bed. In the morning, nothing was charged. The light switch controlled all the power in the room.

We made it to the dealer by 8:00 a.m. Now, we pay more.

THE WEST VIRGINIA FERRY

Lisa arranged the motorcycle trip for my homecoming from a six-month deployment to Afghanistan. It was the second day of our journey, and a misty rain fell on a cool morning. Despite the rain, we were gonna ride. We fired up our two new Moto Guzzi Norges, hit the road, and followed the GPS on a motorcycle route Lisa had heard about.

In my headset, Karen, the GPS voice, announced, "Fr'y in one-quarter mile."

"Lisa," I said, "Fr'y? What's a *fr'y*? I've never heard of a fr'y."

Just then, the road made a right turn, and I didn't, but I didn't land in the woods because I had good brakes. Lisa made the turn and stopped at the bottom of a steep bank at the river's edge. I backed up and turned right to join her.

We were in front of a river ferry, or in GPS Karen–speak, a *fr'y*. This one had a flat wooden deck and a small pilot house on the right side. A cable ran from the shore through rings on the boat's railing to a point on the opposite shore.

A metal ramp connected the road to the ferry. We rode over the slick surface onto the boat and stood by the railing as the pilot ferried us across. We faced another rain-slicked metal plate on the opposite bank.

Lisa went first. Her back tire slid side to side like the road was coated with butter while she struggled to maintain control. My heart stopped. The bike found traction on the concrete, and she shot up the hill—but on the wrong side of the road.

My heart restarted. My turn now. My bike went up like a rocket. At the top, we collected ourselves, then rode on.

THE TREE OF SHAME

The Tail of the Dragon, a short stretch of US Highway 129, runs through the Smoky Mountains and is a bone-breaker, bike-breaker, and heartbreaker. The road draws motorcyclists like a wet T-shirt contest draws party boys at spring break. In 2021 and 2022 alone, there were 123 motorcycle crashes on the stretch, nine of which were fatalities.

So naturally, Lisa wanted to tackle the road on our trip from Pennsylvania to New Mexico, and masochist-me, I agreed. I recall the demonic light in her eyes as she looked at the map. She had visions of exciting twists and turns, while I had visions of shredded parts and fractured limbs. We had just ridden the sedate forty-five-mile-per-hour Blue Ridge Parkway, and now we faced 318 turns in eleven miles.

We picked up the infamous road on the North Carolina side and stopped at Deals Gap Motorcycle Resort to pay homage at the Tree of Shame. We joined fellow motorcyclists in macabre admiration of the collection of shattered bike parts hanging from its limbs. Trashed tanks, fractured fairings, mutilated mufflers, hacked-up handlebars, torn tires, and canes and crutches twisted and sparkled like giant Christmas ornaments in the early afternoon breeze. Handwritten messages adorned the pieces: "Turn 10—broken leg on the crutches." "Turn 13—7/12/05 on the blue fairing." "Turn 7—Too fast on a set of mufflers."

We knew our cruiser-style bikes, with their low-slung frames, were ill-suited for the challenging hairpin turns and serpentine curves, and seeing the tree didn't help.

The road was like the devil's rollercoaster. We rode up and down, left and right, right and left, and down and up. I lost track of space. I lost track of time. I lost track of everything. We reached the end at the Tabcat Creek Bridge.

THE WOODEN BRIDGE

We were on the last leg of a 2,400-mile journey, and we were hungry. Lisa found a mom-and-pop diner close to our route on a questionable two-lane road, as the roads Lisa selects often are.

The road led us to a bridge—not a standard steel-and-concrete bridge, but a wooden bridge—and not just any wooden bridge, but a bridge almost touching the water. With its rough cross-members, it resembled a railroad bridge. Instead of rails, cupped and warped two-by-tens formed the tire tracks.

We decided to chance it and carefully crossed in single file. At the far end, 150 feet from the water's edge, stood a small white structure in the middle of the road, almost as small as a phone booth. As we approached, we saw a pint-sized tin can extend from the window at the end of a wooden dowel.

We stopped at the window.

"Twenty-five cents or fifty cents for the whole day," said the occupant.

It was a toll booth. We were astonished. We paid and, after taking a few photos, left. Once moving, my bike felt a bit squirrely. At the diner, I saw why. The rear tire was almost flat, an apparent victim of the bridge.

Fortunately, a classic car restorer had his shop next door. He inspected the tire and found a slice. It wasn't fixable.

But there was hope. His assistant, a motorcyclist, had a friend who had just bought a motorcycle that came with a spare tire. The spare might fit. After a quick call, the buddy arrived with the tire. I gave him forty dollars for it. The young assistant changed the tire, sparing me the work, but didn't want any money. I gave him sixty dollars for his help, a bargain considering he'd saved our trip.

ST. LOUIS

In the distance, a dark green cloud as wide as the sky roiled and churned, promising a second biblical flood. We rode in staggered formation, Lisa leading, bike motors humming in unison, singing the eternal song of the highway.

"It looks like rain," I said into my communicator, as if the dark sky could mean anything else.

"It's gonna stay to our left," she replied.

But the road curved toward St. Louis and the ominous sky. We stopped under a bridge and donned our rain gear with the fresh scent of ozone in the air.

It felt as if we were riding into a waterfall. Water struck our jackets, ran up our sleeves, bounced off our windscreens, and streaked down our face shields. The wind came in bursts, left and right, and threw us around. Water covered the road, which desperately tried to shed itself of the unwanted coating. On the roadside, ditches filled with water.

We slowed to forty. Cars pulled over to the side of the road, but we could not; the flooded shoulder offered no shelter.

We slowed again, afraid of hydroplaning, as the wind threw water under our tires ... now under thirty ... and then twenty ...

Up ahead, Lisa saw an exit. We took it as if it were the path to the promised land, parked under a bank canopy, and doffed our helmets, glad for the shelter. More refugees from the storm joined us. A Ford Taurus pulled up in the next stall, and a gaggle of giggling teenage girls spilled out. The driver pulled off her wet shoes.

"The windshield leaks," she said.

I looked inside and saw enough water to float a canoe. I was a bit wet, but a motorcycle with a leaky roof still beat a car with a leaky windshield.

LONG-DISTANCE TOOL KIT

What to bring on a long-distance ride:

1. Chamois: Prevents a wet crotch after a rain.
2. Small LED flashlight: Finds that small screw that fell somewhere into the dark recesses of the engine and then under the bike. Valuable even in sunlight.
3. JB Weld: Makes a replacement for the part broken because it was screwed in too tight.
4. Duct tape: I have two rolls. Use this to repair the fairing after the new bike falls over in the parking lot. The tape also reattaches broken turn signals, mirrors, and cracked windshields.

Long-distance tool kit

5. Tire repair kit: Remember the *Why Pay More* incident? Practice using the kit before traveling.

6. Air compressor or CO2 cartridges: Tires go flat on lonely roads, in the rain, and never at a gas station air pump. Ensure the air compressor plugs in and works before traveling. It may also be handy for filling beach balls.

7. Fuses and fuse puller: It seems the bike didn't start because of a broken fuse, not the battery (see No. 8, *multimeter*).

8. Multimeter: Electrical issues occur in hotel parking lots and under roadside bridges, always in the hot sun or driving rain, and never in dry garages. Get a cheap one—you'll probably drop it—about six bucks at Harbor Freight.

9. Medical kit: Get one with plenty of Band-Aids. You know why. Waterproof for hiking/backpacking are the best. Supplement with ibuprofen and Neosporin for skinned knuckles.

10. Zip ties: Fasten broken items in clothing and on the bike.

11. Rubber repair kit: Make leaky repairs to rain gear, dry bags, and luggage.

12. Corkscrew/bottle opener: This is an essential item. Without it, you will push the cork in the bottle, drink all the wine, and wake up late.
13. Boot knife: Looks cool. Never used.

DAVID GODIN

Dave Godin, born and raised in Wisconsin during its ice age, is retired from corporate life and the US Air Force. One day, Dave—wandering lost, still searching for his holy grail, a path to meaningful self-expression—stumbled into a memoir writing class. He was saved and emerged from the class as a writer. Dave is working on his memoir, one short story at a time. He spends his days volunteering; writing; walking his dog, Jake; and driving Lisa, his long-suffering wife of thirty-nine years, to distraction. Recently, *Five Minutes* published Dave's one-hundred-word essay titled "Daily Ritual." Jake says Dave has been impossible to live with ever since.

Every Pawprint Tells a Story

Etya Vaserman Krichmar

VASKA

For some strange reason, every cat in our family was white. The first, Vaska, lived with us for sixteen years, sparking my lifelong love for animals. His snow-white coat had four black socks, two star-like markings above his eyes, and a dark tail. His green eyes, bright with curiosity, and twitching pink nose made me fall in love.

Though independent and a little wild, Vaska was affectionate. He meowed to go outside and hunt each morning, returning through the small window we left ajar. Often, I came home from school to find him basking in the sunlight between the window panes, a freshly caught mouse beside him, his peculiar way of showing love. He kept himself immaculately groomed, licking his fur with the regal air of a creature who knew he ruled his domain.

One day, curious about cats' love for valerian, I placed a few drops on the floor and watched Vaska sniff, lick, and rub his face against the spot. Then, as if overtaken by bliss, he curled into a ball, stretched, and rolled onto his back with his paws in the air. His antics sent me into fits of laughter. For years, sensing my joy, Vaska returned to that spot, reenacting his bizarre ritual with the same ecstatic abandon.

As he aged, his absences grew longer, leaving me uneasy. Then, one day, he returned frail and thin, his once-plush fur hanging loosely over sharp bones. Though weak, his spirit remained unbroken. I bathed him gently, feeling the weight of his decline. That night, he curled beside me, purring a lullaby of love and farewell.

By morning, Vaska was gone. Yet, I still glimpse him in sunlit windows and hear his purr in quiet moments, a reminder that even fleeting love leaves an eternal imprint on the heart.

PAPA'S MYSTERIOUS REX

A scruffy mutt materialized out of nowhere on a warm October evening. Without a bark, he approached, sniffed our arms, and deliberately chose to stay. His small but muscular body bore the scars of battles and neglect, but his eyes, a warm, trusting amber, held a depth that defied his rough exterior.

Canine experts say kindness in a dog's eyes reflects its pedigree. If true, our mutt would have ranked among the noblest breeds, for his heart was pure gold. After he followed us home, Papa, recovering from a massive brain surgery, named him Rex and fed him scraps. From that moment, they were inseparable.

Rex was Papa's shadow for a year, always by his side. Every afternoon, I found Papa stroking Rex's coarse fur, moving his hand rhythmically as if he drew his strength from Rex's unwavering presence. Rex would nuzzle Papa's leg, reassuring him he wasn't alone. Their quiet moments spoke louder than words, each providing solace to the other.

When Papa passed away, Rex's grief was palpable. The high pitch of his whine, a heartbreaking lament, penetrated the cold air of the dark and starless night, announcing his sorrow to the world through the chilly air, echoing the void Papa left behind.

Etya Vaserman Krichmar

After Shiva ended, I searched for Rex. I checked the alleys where strays gathered, questioned neighbors, and called his name into the wind. But he was gone.

His disappearance felt as mystical as his arrival, leaving me to ponder his existence as serendipitous. Our beloved mutt was more than a canine. Rex was a guardian of love and loss, vanishing as mysteriously as he had appeared that October. Mysteries like his weave themselves into the fabric of life, reminding us that some bonds defy explanation and leave us forever changed for having known them.

MAX'S CRIMINAL OFFENSES

In 1992, a golden retriever joined our family in Brooklyn, New York, as a companion for our son after his sister left for college. Initially searching for a black Labrador, we couldn't resist Max's forlorn expression at the pet store, so we brought him home. Inspired by Goofy's son, our son named him Max, short for Maximillian.

Max, criminal offender

Over eight years, Max brought joy and a series of *incidents*. We humorously dubbed them his "criminal offenses." Here are some:

1. The Bitten Hand Incident

A friend touched Max's sore ears, prompting him to nip her hand. No harm was caused, but a complaint was lodged. Police eventually dropped the charges.

Max's defense: "My ears were infected!"

2. The Home Attendant Attack

Max lunged at my mother's home attendant, injuring her arm enough to require an ER visit.

Max's defense: "She stared at me! Even she admitted it provoked me."

3. The Family Scratch

Max scratched our son as he scolded him for breaking a décor piece. We filed no official report.

Max's defense: "He attacked me first. It was self-defense!"

4. The Visitor Incident

Max jumped on my nephew's girlfriend, scratching her leg. A law firm sent a threatening letter claiming the injury disrupted her life.

In Max's defense, we countered with a video showing her dancing and laughing. Case closed.

5. The Trash Bite Quarantine

When Max scavenged in the trash, an argument with our daughter led to a bite and a brief rabies observation quarantine.

In Max's defense, a police officer said, "What's trash to us is food to a dog."

Despite Max's antics and knack for being misunderstood, his goofy, loyal, and spunky personality brought unconditional love to our family. His *offenses* are now cherished memories of a dog who added lessons and laughter to our lives.

THE NOBLE ACE

During one of the loneliest chapters of my life, Ace Heatherwood Flashback, a black Labrador retriever with a pedigree fit for royalty, entered my world. Our son, Jeff, had moved to New York, and shortly after, we lost Max, our beloved golden retriever. The silence in our home was suffocating, a hollow echo of what once was.

Ace's arrival felt like fate. Years earlier, I'd admired a black Lab in Brooklyn, sparking a quiet wish. That memory resurfaced as I searched for a puppy to fill the void Max left. After countless calls, a kind woman in Lakeland, Florida, said, "I've one black Lab left." Three hours later, a bundle of black fur leaped into my arms. It was love at first sight.

Ace's playful antics and calm loyalty brought joy back to our home. One unforgettable day, he struggled to climb out of the pool's deep end, nearly drowning. Determined to help, we heated the pool during the Florida winter and taught him to swim. Soon, he glided effortlessly, his pride shining brighter than the sun.

Ace's intelligence often amazed us, but

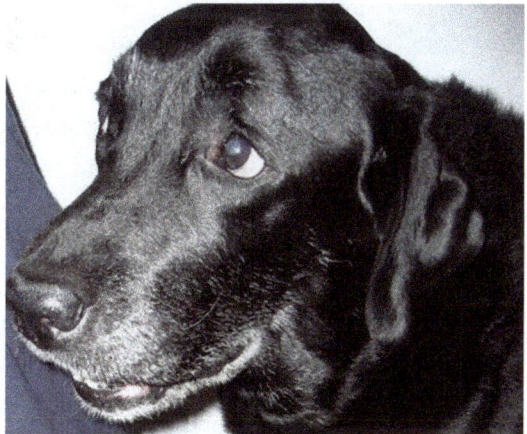

Ace, best dog ever

one moment left us laughing for days. Watching a rerun of his training session on DVD, Ace thought it was real. His tail wagged in anticipation of never-materializing treats, and his confused pout sealed his place as a family comedian.

He wasn't just a dog. Ace was my guardian. During a near-death experience, his quiet presence anchored me. His eyes, filled with unconditional love, told me I wasn't alone.

Though he's gone, his memory lingers. I miss the warmth of his gaze, the softness of his silky coat, the smooches we shared, and the laughter he brought. Ace was family. He taught me that love transcends words and lives in quiet moments where connection needs no explanation.

THE MISCHIEVOUS DUO: MAPLE AND WILLOW

The inseparable duo

What began as a simple trip to Marietta, Georgia, became an adventure that brought us two unexpected bundles of joy: Maple and Willow.

Despite their contrasting personalities—Maple's queenly dignity and Willow's mischievous energy—they complemented each other perfectly, forming an inseparable duo. Maple's steady, watchful nature often balanced Willow's impulsive antics, and together, they filled our home with the harmony only they could create.

We suddenly found ourselves . . .

- Buying crates, playpens, and toys.
- Visiting the vet for a checkup before heading home.
- Worrying about them, especially when each injured their back.

Maple amazed us with her resilience: After narrowly avoiding surgery, she bounced back within days, thanks to steroids. Later, when diabetes stole her sight, she faced it with grace, bravely tolerating three years of insulin shots.

Willow and Maple kept us on our toes, always up to mischief:

- Chasing squirrels and eventually catching one.
- Attacking a snake, with Maple proudly parading it around the yard, victorious.
- Becoming escape artists, digging under the fence.

But beyond the antics, it was their bond that touched us most. Though opposites in personality, they were inseparable, curling up together after every adventure. Once, Maple stood guard while Willow tried to sneak into the pantry, wagging her tail like an accomplice caught in the act. Their teamwork left us laughing for days.

Maple's final moments were serene, a peaceful farewell befitting her regal nature. Now, as Willow approaches her sixteenth birthday, she carries the legacy of their mischievous duo, reminding us every day of the love, laughter, and cherished memories.

The two sisters, small in stature yet huge in presence, have taught us lessons about resilience, perseverance, and determination to get their way—lessons we never expected to learn. They are, and always will be, an irreplaceable part of our family.

BAMBI

Bambi strutted through the house like a king, his tiny frame belying the confidence of a much larger breed. Resembling the cartoon character from *Reindeer*, his wide eyes and delicate legs charmed everyone who met him. But beneath that adorable exterior, Bambi had a mischievous side—he humped everything in sight, utterly unfazed by judgment.

We tolerated his antics, allowing him to sire a litter with a copper-colored Chihuahua. Bambi became the proud father of four pups, cementing his legacy. But after our son was born, his antics escalated. He'd sneak into the nursery to steal pacifiers, prancing away as if he'd found treasure. One winter morning, just as I prepared to take my baby for a walk, I discovered Bambi had peed on my son's blanket. Innocently, he sat by the door, tail wagging as if daring me to scold him. "What are you going to do?" his expression seemed to say.

Balancing a new baby and Bambi's chaos became too much. With heavy hearts, we found him a new home with a breeder. He thrived there, quickly becoming the pack leader, his tiny size no match for his bold spirit. Bambi ruled by sheer confidence, earning his title by dominating every male and female in the pack.

We missed having him, especially his hidden talent for singing. Whenever the right note played, Bambi threw his head back and howled in his high-pitched tone, a soulful serenade that left us laughing. His singing gift, which we never expected, made parting with him even harder.

Our Bambi, a larger-than-life dog, wasn't just a pet; he was a character, a bright, audacious, and full-of-life pup. Though his time with us was short, his attention-grabbing personality left an unforgettable mark on our family, and his memory still makes us smile.

ETYA VASERMAN KRICHMAR,

Where do forgiveness and kindness emanate from in someone who has experienced hate and exclusion?

Etya Vaserman Krichmar, a Soviet refugee, escaped a country of not enough in 1977 to seek freedom in the United States with her husband and two-year-old daughter. Born in Kazakhstan but labeled Jewish by the Soviet regime, Etya was denied faith and identity, enduring relentless antisemitism.

Her struggles and stolen childhood stories are honest, powerful, and profoundly moving. A published author, Etya's work has appeared in *TC Palm*, *Orlando Sentinel*, *The Write Launch*, *Spillwords Press*, *White Rose Magazine*, and *Masticadores-sUSA*, as well as in the anthologies *Turning Points* and *Knocked Sideways*.

Etya is an active member of the Florida Writers Association, Writing Away Refuge, Deadlines for Writers, Memoir Ink, Alumni Café, Pitch to Published, and Athena Sisterhood writing communities. Her writing explores themes of resilience, freedom, and the immigrant experience. Follow her at www.etyawrites.com.

The Losses That Formed Who I Am

Darlene Atkinson Lamb

HEARING THE TRUTH, FINALLY

In October of the year I turned seven, my mother told me she was getting married. Days later, while my friend Lorraine and I were practicing our skipping skills, I decided to tell her the disturbing news.

"My mum's getting married."

"Yeah, I know, she said.

"But there is something I don't understand."

"What?"

"How can she be getting married when she's already married to my dad?"

"Your dad is dead."

My heart stopped. "No, he's not. My mum told me he's just gone away," I whispered.

"Well, my mom told me he died. Let's go and ask her," she suggested.

Lorraine's mother, Ruby, was my mum's friend. We went into the house where she was baking bread, her hands covered in flour, and she asked us what we wanted. I told her my dilemma.

Ruby turned toward me, wiped her floured hands on her apron, and placed them gently on my shoulders. She knelt down, looked me straight in the eye, and said, "Darlene, it's true. Your father is dead. He died when you were four, and you came to live with your grandparents."

Pulling me into her arms with a caring hug, she wiped away my tears with her apron.

My family had never spoken of what they believed were grown-up conversations in my presence. I never saw anyone grieve or cry. About fifty years later, I bravely explained to my mother the grief I had about not being told my father died when he did, and she said, "Oh, we must have told you something."

Yes, she did. She told me he had "just gone away." I lived my life for three years wondering when he was coming back. He never did.

SHE MUST HAVE BIRTHED HERSELF

She arrived unannounced with no fanfare nor greetings. She must have birthed herself. Did they put me to sleep? I have no memory of her being born.

They brought her to me to nurse, then quickly took her away and strapped down my breasts, wrapping them so tightly I could hardly breathe. To stop breathing and die would have been easier. My life was over one way or the other, for you see, it was 1962, and I was an unwed mother.

Three days later, they brought her to me, closed the dark blue curtains for privacy, and told me to say my goodbyes.

She was quiet and seemed content. Her brown eyes held mine as I stared at her in wonder. She didn't know it would be the last time we would be together. I held her close as tears streamed from my eyes. She was so beautiful, so pink. Her tiny fingers held one of mine as I rocked back and forth.

Darlene Atkinson Lamb

With thoughts racing through my mind, I uttered, "I'm sorry. I'm so sorry."

Holding her close to my heart, I whispered a soft "Please forgive me," though I was sure I would never forgive myself. Sobs engulfed me as I watched them carry her away, out of my life forever. I closed my eyes, resigning myself for what I was about to do.

Later that day, adoption papers were brought for me to sign, agreeing to never seek nor contact her. Seeing no alternative, and believing it best for her, I painfully signed.

My heart cracked into a million pieces. I picked up the broken shards, tucked them gently into my blue suitcase between the layers of guilt and shame, left the hospital, and got on the next bus out of town.

THE WEDDING DRESS

It was a simple white wedding dress, the color of perfection. It had a sweetheart neckline, a short-sleeved fitted bodice, and a full-length skirt, the symbol of goodness, innocence, purity, and virginity, but there were a few fake pearls tucked into the bodice.

With her head in a fog, she slowly dressed, placed the tiara with the short, borrowed veil on her head, applied some lipstick, and took a deep breath. Today, she would marry her high school sweetheart. This should be the happiest day of her life—but it wasn't. She knew she was still a good girl, however naive she had been. But her innocence and purity were lost. So was her virginity. And not to the man she would be marrying today.

Her young innocence was stolen by a big-city guy with ideas of his own. Her purity ended on a warm summer's day at a picnic on a blue blanket down by the river. She was no longer a virgin. She was pregnant. When she learned he was married, she knew she was on her own.

She left her job, her friends and moved away. When the baby was born, she surrendered her for adoption, signing papers to never try to be in contact with her again. She picked up the pieces of her broken heart, pretended nothing had happened to her, and kept the secret for her mother's sake.

She left the wedding dress at her mother's house.

ADAM

March 3, 1994, 4:00 a.m.

We awoke when the bedside telephone rang.

My heart skipped a beat. Nobody calls before daylight unless it's an emergency. I picked up the receiver. "Hello?"

I heard Lana's quivering voice. "Mom, please come. We're at the hospital. It's Adam."

Half dazed, asking unanswerable questions, my husband and I dressed quickly, jumped into the car, knowing something was wrong.

Arrived at hospital. Led to private room. Our daughter, her husband, and a hospital chaplain, waiting. Shocked and overwhelmed, Lana fell into our arms while the chaplain explained: Adam has died.

I could feel my heart breaking. *This is not right. Things like this should never happen. A baby dying is beyond comprehension. It's out of order; the older should die first, then the next, never the youngest.* I closed my eyes, shaking my head in disbelief, trying to breathe, to relieve some stress.

"Would you like to see him?" someone asked.

His body lay dressed in his diaper and an undershirt cut open up the front. He was lying there, cold and exposed. I bent over and laid my hand on his wee body in disbelief. He felt like a china doll. *How could this have happened? Someone who was here yesterday and now is gone, and all we are left with is this hardened and ever-so-cold corpse.*

We buried Adam on March 10, 1994, wearing the tiny blue jumpsuit I had knit for him when he was born.

It was snowing, and the north winds blew hard. My memory is of Lana standing next to her father, his arm comforting her as she leaned into him, crying out her grief as they lowered the little white coffin into the frozen ground.

"Ohhh, Daaad . . ."

HIM, ME, AND THE ELEPHANTS

An invisible blue elephant began following me around when I realized I was pregnant, unmarried, and alone.

I told my mother and my boyfriend (who wasn't the father) the truth.

Three months following the birth and surrendering of the baby, I accepted the boyfriend's proposal of marriage, and three months later we were married. My mother was happy. No one spoke nor took notice of the blue elephant.

While my husband climbed the ladder of success, I was to stay home to make life easier for him and our three children, doing all the things no one else wanted to do—and be grateful.

To the outside world, the husband acted the extrovert—charming, outgoing, kind, helpful. Inside, his true introvert sucked all the energy out of me. He was uncommunicative, selfish, and demanding. I became successful at feeling guilty, unworthy, and never good enough.

His ego's addiction for success caused stress, which he treated with alcohol, leaving him a workaholic and a functioning hidden alcoholic. There were now two blue elephants strolling through his house under invisible cloaks.

My tiny inner light fought to stay alive while he frantically denied his own mid-life crises. He chose to find another woman to save while he reclaimed his youth and forced me to leave his home.

In our almost forty years together as a couple, we never spoke about the elephants. He never understood we were living with unacknowledged issues that caused our unhappiness. If we had spoken, it might have made a world of difference. Blue elephants are hard to live with.

THE REST OF THE STORY

The previous five stories were kept on hold until the time was right for my readiness to share. The intention for the sixth is to tell the rest of the story.

I filled volumes of journals, attended sessions with numerous therapists, read self-help books, attended healing retreats and conferences, traveled, photographed, studied, and put in the hard inner work, getting the results necessary to have the desire to continue living. Reaching a place of peace, I am now able to function as a spiritual, loving being living a human life.

I was able to connect on a higher-dimensional level with members of my family, those who had died and those who have chosen to abandon me. I learned my father adored and loved me. I came to believe that perhaps my father and baby Adam have the same soul.

My creative life began when the marriage broke up. A photograph I took after Adam died, titled *The Gift*, became well known, and proceeds enabled me to travel and also reunite with the baby I surrendered for adoption. Our thirty-eight-year relationship still flourishes. Her first words to me when we met were, "Thank you for giving me life."

I would have stayed in the loveless marriage forever, honoring my wedding promises, but I see now that his leaving me for another woman was the best gift my husband ever gave me. Was this a cosmic gift of love? Perhaps. I picked myself up and began seeing the strong woman I really am.

The loss of connection with the children from the marriage is still a mystery. Their father let them to believe I was the one who left and dissolved the family. With great sadness, I have let them go. If they are mine, they will return.

DARLENE ATKINSON LAMB

During the 1980s, Darlene Lamb attended International Women's Writing Guild conferences where she learned the words of Florida Scott-Maxwell: "You need only claim the events of your life to make yourself yours. When you truly possess all you have been and done, which may take some time, you are fierce with reality."[12]

For Darlene Lamb, this indeed did take some time—forty years, in fact. She lives in Guelph, Ontario, Canada, and is happy to report in her eighty-sixth year: She has claimed these events of her life and is now truly "fierce with reality."

---

[12] Florida Scott-Maxwell, *The Measure of My Days*, New York: Alfred A. Knopf, Inc., 1973, p. 27.

Holly's Days
Holly Martinez

UNPACK THE SANTA SUIT

In 2006, my daughter-in-law Maria organized a community event sponsored by her law firm to promote child safety. She arranged for Santa to arrive in a fire truck to surprise the children, including her toddler daughter, Kaylee.

Maria had heard stories about my husband, Felix, the bilingual Santa. Knowing he owned a Santa suit inspired her idea: She asked Felix (Papa) to dress up as Santa, ride in the fire truck, and wave and talk to the children.

He happily agreed.

Kaylee and her Papa Santa

Kaylee

Many children lined up to have their pictures taken and fingerprints printed onto identification safety cards.

As time passed, Kaylee's twinkling eyes began to close, and her smile faded. Maria asked me to hand her to Papa so she could ride around and nap on his lap.

One little girl saw me give Kaylee to Papa, and I overheard her say, "Wow, that little girl is really lucky. She knows Santa."

Now that the Santa suit came out of storage, I had an idea. I scheduled a photo shoot with Papa wearing the Santa suit and holding his cheerful, smiling granddaughter, Kaylee, with her big brown eyes.

That is how the first traditional yearly Santa picture began.

SANTA IS COMING

I had just turned five in the early 1950s. My parents took me to the Lions Club Christmas party, where my father was the president.

The children gathered in the assembly hall, eagerly awaiting Santa's arrival. When Santa walked in the door, their eyes lit up. They clapped, cheered, and bounced up and down. He waved his large hand, covered in a white glove. "Ho ho ho!" he exclaimed as he strolled to the front of the room, pulling his giant red sack behind him. Santa settled into a large, Santa-sized chair and picked up the microphone. One by one, he called each child by name to come to the front.

It felt like ages, but finally, he called my name. I skipped up the aisle, my blond braids bouncing from side to side as I went to meet him.

He spoke into the microphone. "Holly, I have these paper dolls for you—"

Holly Martinez

"Thank you, Santa." I quickly took them from his hand. "Thank you."

Santa continued, saying, "—if you promise not to suck your thumb anymore."

I thought about it for a moment before handing him the paper dolls. "Santa, you can keep the dolls. I'll keep my thumb." Then I ran back to my mom as fast as I could.

Later that night, my dad took me aside when we got home. Tearfully, he revealed that he had dressed up as Santa. He hugged me and apologized for embarrassing me.

Now, much to my sadness, I realized no Santa was sneaking down the chimney, and there would be no paper dolls for me. I felt like I had disappointed my parents. But I quietly slipped my favorite thumb into my mouth when I went to bed that night. My thumb has never, ever disappointed me.

GOODBYE, SANTA

I didn't realize my Christmas at seven would be my last until I met Grandma Soledad Martinez eighteen years later.

My mother became involved with a cult that preached that Christmas—along with all other holidays and events outside its beliefs—was worldly and forbidden. They branded these practices as sins and labeled them pagan. The leader manipulated people and instilled deep fear in her followers.

Due to what the cult leader deemed as her unacceptable worldly beliefs, I was forcibly kept isolated and hidden from my dad from the age of seven until I was twelve years old.

I learned a lot by observing the leader's schemes and her exploitation of innocent people.

The leader proclaimed my destiny was to marry her son at eighteen.

However, her plan backfired when, at eighteen, I discovered I was pregnant by the boy who lived across the street. Since he wasn't part of the church compound, the cult excommunicated me.

There are no mistakes. My freedom from the cult and my survival were blessings.

I knew I carried gifts within me, liberated from their grasp. I held these gifts close to my heart because I felt love, compassion, care, and truth inside me, which starkly contrasted with the cult's teachings. They failed to recognize these gifts.

My happiness didn't depend on Christmas or external influences—there were no presents, decorations, or insincere people. I didn't need a pretender in a Santa suit to convince me I needed a store-bought gift. I never subscribed to the Santa myth or misled my children about it.

Instead, I taught them we all possess God-given light and energy within us and should actively honor and treasure this awareness.

This was my gift.

GRANDMA SOLEDAD'S GIFT

On Christmas Eve, I clung tightly to my boyfriend's arm as we climbed the creaky wooden stairs blanketed with snow and frozen slush. "What if they don't like me?"

"You? My blond bombshell? They'll adore you."

When my boyfriend opened the door, the sounds of a mariachi guitar and a flurry of warm hugs and kisses greeted us. The serenades and vibrant scene—a black leather bar, a floor-to-ceiling gold mirror reflecting colorful red-and-gold flocked wallpaper, a pink-and-turquoise floral carpet, an impressive winding staircase, and a Felix the Cat clock wagging its tail on the wall—overwhelmed me.

In front of the staircase stood a two-story Christmas tree adorned with shockingly bright red, orange, purple, and green ornaments.

Hidden among the branches was a maddeningly loud squawking bird.

Every year at eight p.m., a knock signaled Santa's arrival as he walked in with his sacks of goodies.

⁊⦿

Seven years later, nothing had changed. This year, Grandma had Santa give her fourteen grandchildren and great-grandchildren ingenious space blasters. Each gun emitted loud, annoying sounds and multicolored lights that flashed in sync with the clattering of the blaster. Before long, the house erupted into joyful chaos. The children dashed up and down the grand staircase, past Grandma, and through the kitchen, dining room, and living room in endless loops of laughter and flashing lights.

Glancing at Grandma Soledad Martinez, seated in her gold-and-royal-blue chair, clapping her frail fingers as she watched her family play and laugh, I saw when she turned to me, placed her shaking hands on her heart, smiled proudly, and said, "These are all my childrens. I love them."

This was her gift, a home filled with love and joy.

I learned the true meaning of Christmas from her: family, love, and joy.

THE 2024 LETTER

2024. What I've learned this year:

Be thankful for every moment.

Never take not even a second for granted.

When we lose someone we love, we must learn not to live without them but to live with the love they left behind.

I'm blessed to have had Felix/Chino/Papa for forty-seven years.

Now, I'm learning to reinvent Holly. A Holly I didn't even realize existed with just myself.

This is all new to me.

What do I do about so many things without Papa here by my side? What about the tools, sculptures, canes, and traditional Papa Santa/family pictures?

Do I pack away Papa's Santa suit, gift it to another Santa, or hand it down to his legacy and keep the tradition going?

Memories you create and share define life. They're all you leave behind.

Life is more than just this moment.

Count your life by smiles and by friends. Count not the years but the life you live.

A fellow buddy writer wrote and sent me this. These words gave me the moxie and endurance to continue: "No one else I know smiles the way you do. You live a life with lots of good and hard. Every time I see you, you're in the game. There's no waiting around for Holly. You seize today."

Smile at others. Speak kind words. You never know the effect they have on someone else.

Despite Felix's death—and Martin County's death-defying tornados, hurricanes, and the weakening of my skylight —I remain standing.

Be the shining-light thread in the beautiful tapestry of the world. Make each year the best year and enjoy your ride.

I love my journey.

I thank you for supporting me through my voyage, whether you are near or far. You intensify my heart and my soul.

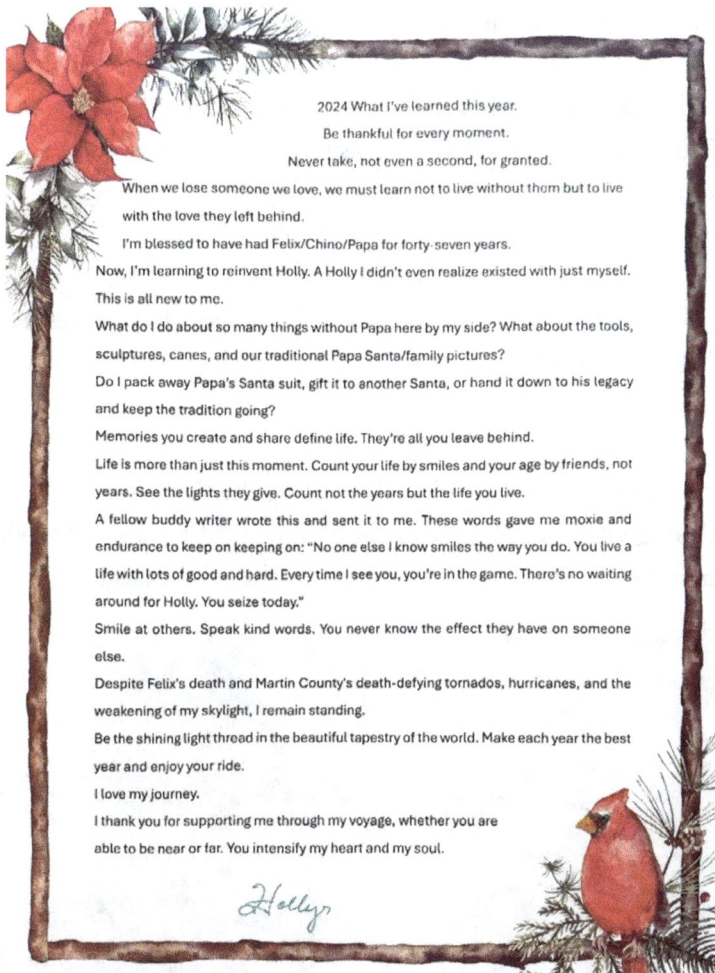

2024 What I've learned this year.

Be thankful for every moment.

Never take, not even a second, for granted.

When we lose someone we love, we must learn not to live without them but to live with the love they left behind.

I'm blessed to have had Felix/Chino/Papa for forty-seven years.

Now, I'm learning to reinvent Holly. A Holly I didn't even realize existed with just myself. This is all new to me.

What do I do about so many things without Papa here by my side? What about the tools, sculptures, canes, and our traditional Papa Santa/family pictures?

Do I pack away Papa's Santa suit, gift it to another Santa, or hand it down to his legacy and keep the tradition going?

Memories you create and share define life. They're all you leave behind.

Life is more than just this moment. Count your life by smiles and your age by friends, not years. See the lights they give. Count not the years but the life you live.

A fellow buddy writer wrote this and sent it to me. These words gave me moxie and endurance to keep on keeping on: "No one else I know smiles the way you do. You live a life with lots of good and hard. Every time I see you, you're in the game. There's no waiting around for Holly. You seize today."

Smile at others. Speak kind words. You never know the effect they have on someone else.

Despite Felix's death and Martin County's death-defying tornados, hurricanes, and the weakening of my skylight, I remain standing.

Be the shining light thread in the beautiful tapestry of the world. Make each year the best year and enjoy your ride.

I love my journey.

I thank you for supporting me through my voyage, whether you are able to be near or far. You intensify my heart and my soul.

Holly

My 2024 Letter

IN HONOR OF FELIX MARTINEZ

We took annual photos without our beloved Felix—my husband, Dad, Papa, Santa—yet we still upheld the tradition.

My children came to celebrate my birthday during the first week of December. I organized our annual photo session, carefully planning outfit changes and capturing countless images.

The photos included Holly's birthday, Kaylee's Christmas, and a family picture with our pets and Santa. However, after eighteen years of this cherished tradition, we no longer had Felix to keep it alive. There wasn't a Papa to wear the Santa suit.

I asked the children, "What should we do?"

They all shared the same sentiment: "I don't know."

I called Kaylee's dad, Jonah, for advice. He suggested, "Mom, bring the picture of Dad and Kaylee's first Santa suit photo."

Great idea!

He also recommended that I bring the Santa suit. I sifted through drawers and stacks of photos until I found Kaylee's first picture with her Papa Santa. I gathered the jacket, pants,

Eighteen-year-old Kaylee Felicia, holding the framed photo
of herself and her Papa

Felix (ninety-one years old) and Holly's
forty-seventh wedding anniversary

Holly with son, Jonah;
granddaughter, Kaylee; and Roadie

boots, belt, gloves, and hat, packing them all into a bag to take with us.

It broke our hearts to face the first celebration without our Felix, Dad, Papa.

For Kaylee's photo this year, she held her Papa's picture, which added a lovely touch.

After we took all the pictures on the list, Jonah reached into the bag and put on Papa's Santa jacket and hat. He transformed into half-Santa and half-Jonah. What a beautiful tribute.

We took our family picture with tears as Jonah changed into the spirit of Santa/Dad.

I'm uncertain about this year's Christmas spirit but feel deeply grateful.

My gift is having such heartfelt children.

—*In memory and honor of Felix Martinez.*

HOLLY MARTINEZ

Holly Martinez began writing at eleven years old, since the day her beloved Aunt Evie said, "Write a book. You have a story to tell."

Holly is working on her third manuscript, "One Soul, Three Contracts," based on her anything-but-normal life. She believes she agreed to a predetermined plan before entering this life. Everything in life happens for a set reason, and no accidents occur. Even if her mind can't see the explanation.

Holly lives in Palm City, Florida. She is a member of Life Writers and the Palm City Write Club.

Welcome to the Country

Linda Monnahan Peterson

THE MOVE TO DEER CREEK

In April 1968, when I was just a young thing, two days after the assassination of Dr. Martin Luther King Jr., I married and moved to the tightly knit little farming community of Deer Creek on the Minnesota-Iowa border.

All that was left of the former village at that time was the vacant store on the Iowa side of the state line, as well as the abandoned cheese factory, the cheesemaker's house, and the Deer Creek Valley Lutheran Church on the Minnesota side.

My new husband, Gordon, had spent the last eighteen years of his life in this area. He—and his older brother, Arnold, with whom he farmed—traded baling, corn shelling, and heavier farming tasks with close neighbors.

My introduction to the neighborhood happened two days after our wedding, when Gordon's brother showed up, looking for a cup of coffee and farm talk. Forget lounging around in my bathrobe, I guess.

That was followed a couple of days later by a contingent of Gordon's large family descending on us to help Gordon celebrate his twenty-fifth birthday.

Later that week, a groomsman at our wedding appeared on our doorstep, looking for assistance. His car had broken down on his way to work. Three days later, he was followed by an elderly man showing up, trying to sell me tree seedlings. Only after I had tried to give him the bum's rush—*Doesn't he notice our heavily wooded acreage?*—did I notice Gordon visiting with him out in the yard.

"Didn't you recognize Sam, the former storekeeper?" he asked. After closing the store, Sam had become an arborist on wheels. He had sold new trees to everyone in a ten-square-mile area.

So much for a crash course to my new community.

FARM LIFE 101

While, admittedly, I went into marriage with stars in my eyes, I very quickly had them plucked out by . . .

1. Realizing we lived a quarter mile away from our nearest neighbor and ten miles from anywhere I could buy groceries.

2. Having my brother-in-law, Gordon's farming partner, show up at our place—needed or not—at least twice a day, often early in the morning.

3. Discovering that, during crop season, I was expected to deliver coffee—along with sandwiches and something sweet—twice a day, wherever in the field the guys were working. This was in addition to, not in lieu of, providing three squares a day.

4. Learning to do farm bookwork. Using a farm account book provided by the local elevator (no computers back then), I had to keep track of receipts for everything purchased or sold.

5. Ditto learning to drive a four-on-the-floor, straight-stick 1952 pickup with side boards, following the combine around the field on a cold November day, while we finished harvesting the wet spots in the soybean field.

6. Watching my seventy-year-old mother-in-law slide into dementia. While also . . .
7. Losing my own mother on New Year's Eve morning of that same year as my seven sisters and I circled her hospital bed reciting the Lord's Prayer.
8. Welcoming my thirteen-year-old sister to live with us after my mother's death.
9. Learning, as we neared our first anniversary, that we were to become parents. That rounded out our first year.

FREAK-OUT!

In our second year of marriage, I got the opportunity to meet the rest of Gordon's large family. Not the last of them was Belean, his oldest sister. Like him, she was short, stocky, and dark-haired.

She, her husband, gray-haired, bespectacled Ronald, and sixteen-year-old twins, David and Debbie, rolled off the gravel road into the driveway at Arnold's farm. They parked directly across the crushed-rock driveway from the front door of the farmhouse.

Of course, Arnold let us know we should come over to greet them.

Ronald was an alcoholic retired US Navy NCO. He wanted everything around him to be shipshape while he sat in their trailer, nursing his brandy into oblivion. By the time we arrived at Arnold's, Ronald had unhitched the trailer from the car, leveled it, and driven the car close to the nearest water hydrant. With a hose, he sprayed off every inch of the vehicle, including what was under the hood.

I am sure he gave me the expected proper greeting when we were introduced, but I don't remember much of anything else about him except how Belean danced around him, catering to his every whim, trying to keep him from popping a cork. This did not sit well with my mother-in-law, who told her, "Let him wait on his damn self!"

Another memory from that visit comes to mind. David and my sister, Denise, didn't waste any time connecting with each other. One day, with everyone gathered here, they decided to take a walk to the nearby creek. When his parents found both missing, they went into full freak-out mode, hollering the young couples' names, thinking the worst.

Before long, either due to hearing all the commotion or of their own volition, the young couple returned, unharmed.

AND BABY MAKES THREE

We continued to be challenged by raising swine against a backdrop of an, as yet, unidentified disease problem. We hauled gallon after gallon of red-tinted antibiotics out of the veterinarian's office. This was mixed into our hundred-gallon watering tanks, to be consumed by the growing pigs, to keep *the scours* at bay. We were always diligent to withdraw this medicine on time so as not to contaminate the meat as the animals went to market.

Amid this and the concern over the growing crops, I was becoming increasingly excited about our baby-to-be. Sometime that summer, I began to embroider a quilt top in a nursery rhyme motif—Jack and Jill, Little Bo Peep, and other characters. As I anticipated having a boy, I finished the quilt in a pale blue binding.

As summer rolled into fall, after harvesting the oats, the men decided their old pull-type Allis Chalmers combine would not make it through the heavier harvest season. They traded it in on a used IHC 303 self-propelled model.

With my due date in view, we decided it was a good idea to install a telephone. The first calls made on that phone were in search of parts for the Allis when it broke down with amazing regularity.

Although I did not want a baby shower until the baby arrived, I was honored at one given by my sister-in-law Jenny in the last week of October. This event outfitted us with everything we needed for our bundle of joy, including cloth diapers.

Michelle, our bald, hazel-eyed little beauty, arrived three weeks past her due date, just a day shy of her Grandma Peterson's seventy-second birthday. She and I came home to a welcoming committee of Grandma and Arnold.

They were served coffee before they left that night.

THE 1970S

The 1970s were eventful here, to say the least. To begin with, we began the year adoring our brand-new baby girl. Before the year was out, my sister Denise moved out to live with one of our older sisters.

With Gordon's mother's worsening dementia, she saw me as a threat. She accused me of stealing things from her, most importantly her baby. She became my charge when the guys were in the field or otherwise occupied. She followed me around like a stalker with a silly grin on her face and her hands crossed behind her back.

I stuffed my feelings enough to become a walking time bomb. Migraine headaches became frequent companions.

In 1971, we learned we were expecting an addition to our family.

Meanwhile, our livestock production problems continued. At one time, giving no thought to the widespread transmissible gastroenteritis, or TGE, outbreak at the time, the local vet told us he thought our herd had "a touch of cholera." That was enough to cause trembling in the most stalwart.

With this news, and at the urging of a dairy farmer friend, in 1971, Gordon bought sixteen springing Holstein heifers, due to freshen in the winter. We still had stanchions and other milking equipment left in our barn by the previous owner, as well as milker buckets left from before the 1967 tornado, which had wiped out the brothers' milking operation at the time.

As the truck backed up to the barn with the precious cargo inside, we looked forward to our next enterprise.

DAIRYING AND A NEWBORN SON

Since first-calf heifers are notorious for kicking while learning to be milked, I was forbidden to go into the barn behind the cows as they were stanchioned for milking. I could, however, set up the milk cans and strainer in our makeshift milk room to receive the milk from the buckets after they were filled. At that time, we sold grade B milk.

I also loved feeding the baby calves and teaching them to drink from a pail. Not so much stirring up the milk replacer that served as their feed. No matter how hard I tried to incorporate the dry powder into warm water, I could never rid the stuff of its lumps. The calves did not care, though. Once taught to drink, they slurped it up in no time.

On a snowy night in January, one of our cows was having a tough time giving birth to her calf. The vet was called. Between him and Gordon pulling the calf, something that's done in extreme situations, things turned out all right—for the cow and the calf, that is. While helping with this chore, Gordon tore up muscles in his chest and back so badly, he was thought, days later, to have had a heart attack.

We left for the hospital to have our baby the next morning. The day was cold. The roads and our yard were so icy—we slid into the side of the garage while leaving. Hours later, our son came into the world. I was so excited; I bet I could be heard exclaiming, "It's a boy!" all the way down the hallway from the delivery room, even though it was the middle of the night.

This was only the end of January.

LINDA PETERSON

Linda Peterson, a retired farmwife from far–South Central Minnesota, can see Iowa across the road from her home. She has been writing since elementary school, when she wrote a small booklet of poetry for her class. Her teacher typed it, mimeographed it, and distributed it to her classmates. That was followed later, when, in her young married life, she wrote a farm humor column, The Frazzled Farm Wife, for her local newspaper. A story from that column, "The Hog Sorting Blues," was published in *The National Hog Farmer*.

In later years, Linda became interested in genealogy and, as a result, also in writing her life story, while again dabbling in poetry. She won a small award when her poem "If I Was a Car, My Owner Would Junk Me" was published.

She has been aided, no small amount, in the memoir-writing endeavor by Writing Your Life.

Chapters of a Wonderful Faith-Filled Childhood
Strength Through Faith
Jacqueline Wenger Raymond

KNOWING GOD BEFORE MY EARTHLY EXISTENCE

Early in my existence, I knew Him, my best friend, God. In October 1932, He gathered me in His arms, placed me in my earthly mother's body, and assured me that He would always walk beside or carry me. He kissed my forehead and disappeared.

Time passed. I was rolled up in a ball, cozy and warm.

Often, I heard a sweet, soft voice mingled with a voice that sounded like my friend's, laughing and saying, "Wow! That was a big kick."

Tender rubbings over my body, especially as I stretched and rolled around, comforted me. I was getting bigger and needed more room. Suddenly, I was upside down. My head and body slid down into a tunnel. Movement was difficult. My shoulders were squeezed, and my legs were stretched upward.

My friend's voice whispered, "This is the big day when your mother will take over your care. Know I will always be by your side. Be brave. Push hard with your legs."

My mother and father with
me at my baptism

My mother's body squeezed me extra hard. Suddenly, I saw a bright light. I was out of that little, tight space, and I could stretch.

A deep voice bellowed, "Grab her!"

The nurse held me upside down by my feet and slapped my back. I coughed out something and began screaming.

The doctor said, "Melba, you have a beautiful little dark-curly-haired girl with a powerful set of lungs. She's perfect, two arms with hands and five fingers, two legs with five toes on each foot."

My friend leaned over my mother and whispered, "Take care of my little girl. I will always be here to help."

As my life progressed, God was always there guiding me.

Mother and Father had me baptized at Calvary Episcopal Church at six weeks of age.

MY LIFE AS AN ONLY CHILD

Never regret a day in your life.
Good days give happiness; bad days give experiences;
worst days give lessons; best days give memories.

Being an only child had disadvantages and advantages. I had difficulties bonding with friends. On the plus side, I had parents whose unconditional love, godly faith, and guidance—firm and unwavering—laid the foundation of who I am today and what I have accomplished as a wife, mother, and grandmother. Mother and Father treated me as an adult child, taking me to dances and grown-up activities. My babysitters were aunts and grandparents.

Together, they told me the *facts of life*.

Mother—five feet, two inches tall, 105 pounds—the second of seven children, had curly auburn hair. At eighteen, she had to work to support her widowed mother and five younger brothers while finishing high school and earning her diploma. She groomed me to get a college degree and be a loving, forgiving mother.

My father—five feet, nine inches tall, with wavy black hair—the tenth of twelve children, was a gifted storyteller. I had visual reading problems, dyslexia. Dad nurtured my auditory skills and love for adventure, telling me hundreds of treasured stories. He taught me to sing duets; dance the waltz, jitterbug, and Charleston; and grow vegetables.

Camp Washington Elementary School's education was excellent. Also, from fifth to eighth grade, I sang alto in the choir and played a trumpet in their band. (In the eighth grade, as first chair trumpeter, I played as the flag was raised in the morning and lowered in the afternoon.)

The bell-clanging streetcars carried schoolchildren on field trips. On Sundays, for twenty-five cents, they took people to the different museums, the symphony hall, and the zoo, where on weekends in the summer, operas performed in their open-air theater.

AGE FOUR, MY FIRST ADVENTURE WITH MY DOG, SPOT

When I was four, I embarked on my first adventure with my best friend, Spot, a spirited two-foot-high, black-and-white furry bundle of energy.

My father, a gifted storyteller, filled my young mind with tales of "Hansel and Gretel," "The Boy Who Saved Holland," and other adventures that sparked my thirst for exploration.

It had rained all morning, leaving the backyard coated in mud, perfect for making mud pies. Spot, however, had other ideas. His tail wagged furiously as he dug an escape hole under the white picket fence. He looked at me with his eager doggy grin as if to say, "Come on, Jackie, help me! Let's get goodies at Daddy's store!"

Excited, I dropped to my knees and dug alongside him. Mud smeared my face and new flowered dress as we squeezed under the fence and set off.

Spot, Father, Jackie, and our car

I sang Shirley Temple's "On the Good Ship Lollipop" while Spot barked along. Our unusual duet filled the neighborhood air.

By the grace and, I am sure, the guidance of God, we triumphantly reached Daddy's Kroger grocery store and marched straight to the candy counter.

"I'd like a big lollipop," I announced proudly, "and Spot wants a gooey chocolate!"

Suddenly, a booming voice echoed, "WHAT ARE YOU AND SPOT DOING HERE WITHOUT YOUR AUNTS?"

Spot and I froze, hearing my father's thunderous tone resonating throughout the store.

Later, when Daddy's panic subsided, and Spot and I had served our much-deserved housebound punishment, he crafted a playful ditty about the incident:

My father was a butcher.
My mother cut the meat.
And I was the little wiener wurst
that ran around the street.

CAMP WASHINGTON ELEMENTARY SCHOOL

At age ten, in fifth grade, I picked up my schoolbooks and trumpet case and yelled goodbye to Grandma, Grandpa, and Aunt Marie on my way out, singing, "Onward Christian soldiers, going as to war, with the cross of Jesus going on before . . ."

Our church said that while singing these words, God protected us from the devil's wickedness. I felt protected from the cars, trucks, streetcars, and devils cluttering the three miles of Colerain Avenue I trudged to and from Camp Washington Elementary School Mondays to Fridays, September through May.

My father loved this section of Cincinnati. As the tenth of twelve first-generation German Americans born and raised here, Dad taught me to be fearless. To embrace life with its adventures. He pretended to put little sensory eyes all over me to help me notice bad things around me. I avoided imminent danger.

Over the next six years, I, too, learned to cherish Camp Washington's sights, sounds, and awesome smells flowing from the White Castle hamburgers, Camp Washington Chili parlor, and Grippo's potato chip factory; I even tolerated the nauseating smells emanating from the slaughterhouses.

On weekends, we had fun going to movies for ten cents and buying five-cent candy. On Sundays, for twenty-five cents, we took the streetcars to the Cincinnati Zoo, museums, or the riverboat to Coney Island.

Camp Washington School, built in 1881, offered excellent education from kindergarten through eighth grade, plus a shop for non-academic students. It had superb programs in math, English, science, social studies, and two electives. I chose choir, singing alto, and band, playing a trumpet. These music electives unleashed my genetic links to my mother's grandparents' classical music successes.

In 1954, I received a bachelor's degree in biology. In 1973, a master's degree in elementary education enhanced my teaching.

1946 TO 1950, HIGH SCHOOL YEARS

Hughes High School was larger than my elementary school. When I entered the front door, atop six wide white marble steps stood an immense white marble angel-like statue. I was convinced God placed it there as my guardian angel. Because Hughes was located across from the University of Cincinnati, it had a college atmosphere. I loved it.

It happened in February 1948, my sophomore year. My father, shaking off tons of snow, soot-laden, announced, "This is the last winter I'll shovel snow. We're moving back to Miami this summer."

In June 1948, we sold our house and furniture, packed our two-door, dark-blue Chevrolet coupe with clothes, pots, pans, and a ton of canned goods, and moved to Miami, Florida.

Winged Victory of Samothrace

My life drastically changed. The warm weather was great.

Hughes High School, Cincinnati, Ohio

My parents bought a small two-bedroom house. I had my own bedroom, a first.

The start of school arrived. Alone, scared, I ventured forth.

Miami Jackson's three-story-tall building had its classroom doors open to an outside walkway. Students sat on benches in the courtyard below.

Hughes High School had been collegiately fashionable. My light-gray, heavy-cotton straight skirt with slanted pockets had an inch and a half outward fold, a cuff at the hemline, simple white puffed sleeves, and a scooped neckline. I looked out of place.

Miami Jackson students did not seem to notice. By the end of the first week, all seemed to accept me unconditionally. I was welcomed into the *in* group. As the year progressed, my life got even better. The social activities of the school were geared to academically enhance the college-bound students if they so desired.

By the end of my junior year, the student body elected me vice president of the senior class. I was a cheerleader and in the National Honor Society. Life was good.

MY COLLEGE YEARS AND MARRIAGE

My transfer to the University of Miami from Florida State University was due to my mother's near-death experience from a ruptured stomach ulcer. I was not told about this until they were certain she would live. By God's grace, she did. It was the spring of my sophomore year, 1952, in Florida State. Everything was great: An FSU Village Vamp, I'd joined Kappa Alpha Theta sorority and been elected by the student body to FSU's judicial system. I was a cheerleader in my freshman year; however, my inability to do flips exited me in my sophomore year.

I felt the need to be a watchdog for my mother. Leaving my successes behind, I transferred to the University of Miami to finish college.

God had a different plan for me.

U of M was quite different from Florida State. No chapter of my sorority, no university-elected office. I knew some younger boys from Miami Jackson High School. Being a good listener, we became "only" good friends. They belonged to Kappa Alpha Fraternity. At the end of my junior year, they selected me as their "Sweetheart."

During the year, I was flagged by the University of Miami's newspaper as a "Hurricane Honey." My picture was posted on the front of the school newspaper. In September of my senior year, at the first Kappa Alpha Fraternity Rush Party, I met Norman, a Kappa Alpha from the University of Florida returning from Korean War active duty.

We plan. God laughs.

August 27, 1955, Norman and I married, and my single life evolved into a new adventure as a wife, then mother of five beautiful children—two boys and three girls—and now

June 22, 2022, my ninetieth birthday party

grandmother to eleven wonderful grandchildren—two girls and nine boys, all ages, sixteen to twenty-six (all single, no great-grandchildren).

JACQUELINE WENGER RAYMOND

Jacqueline "Jackie" Wenger Raymond was born and raised in Cincinnati, Ohio. When she was sixteen, her family moved to Miami, Florida, where she finished high school and attended Florida State University and the University of Miami, where she received a BA degree in zoology. She taught elementary school for thirty years, during which time she earned an MBA in elementary education that enhanced her teaching.

At age sixty-seven in 1999, she and her late husband, Norman, began a second career managing their jewelry kiosk businesses at Universal Studios in Orlando, Florida.

Jackie has five children and eleven grandchildren. She has enjoyed ballroom dancing, singing in choirs, and embarking on adventures traveling around the world. Now, she is writing about those things. She published a story, "Dance Steps on the Sea," in the book *Turning Points*.

She has lived in Florida; St. Simons Island, Georgia; and Texas. She now resides in Atlanta, Georgia, with her daughter Darby.

Disheartening Times in My Life

John Roche

TECH SERGEANT TENZA

This vignette is about one of the first serious lessons I learned in my adult life. I failed out of college after my freshman year and had a critical decision to make. The year, 1966. The era, Vietnam War. My two choices included getting drafted or dodging the draft. I chose the latter by signing up with the US Air Force.

I remember strolling down Flatbush Avenue on a mild spring afternoon to the Junction—Flatbush and Nostrand Avenues in Brooklyn, New York—where I entered the US Air Force recruiting office and inquired about becoming an airman. I won't get into details, but those recruiting sergeants are good—promiscuously good. After thirty minutes with my own personal recruiter, Technical Sergeant Tommy Tenza, I couldn't wait to get to basic training—which included swimming pools, modern gymnasiums, all the women I could love, and all the draft beer I could drink at several on-base clubs. Tenza guaranteed it.

Four months later, I completed basic training and the Air Police Academy. The time spent at Lackland Military Training Facility near San Antonio, Texas, was extremely painful and shocking to my system. No pools, no fancy gymnasiums, no beer-guzzling orgies with the WAFs—Women's Air Force. In fact, the only *luxuries* at Lackland were the infrequent breaks at the soda machines and smoke breaks. I didn't smoke until I started basic training. It was one of the few freedoms that existed. I bought a pack of cigarettes; I wasn't going to let the smokers get an edge on me.

During those 120 days of misery, a recurring thought went through my mind. *I can't wait to get back to Brooklyn to kick Tommy's ass.*

THE GRANDFATHER CLAUSE

April 1974. Fate struck me. As a new resident of western Pennsylvania, driving near Pittsburgh International Airport, a sign caught my eye:

911TH TACTICAL AIRLIFT GROUP
UNITED STATES AIR FORCE RESERVE

No way, I thought. *I really hated active duty. Why would I even consider this?*

I turned into the driveway. An hour later, I became one of eighteen members of the 911th Weapons System Security Flight, or WSSF, entering a world that would eventually dictate my career.

Commissioned as a second lieutenant in 1978, I assumed command of the flight and my buddies—not an easy task. One of my former supervisors, M.Sgt. John Stapinski, now worked for me. I often described John as the best damn staff sergeant in the Air Force. He was *grandfathered* to master sergeant because of time served. John had one minor flaw. He was a worthless supervisor. Inspectors always gigged the flight because of a weak link; that link was John.

I eventually had a decision to make, so I had John transferred to civil engineers, where he would be harmless and finish his career. John didn't understand that I could have terminated him.

John did not choose the high road. He went on the attack. He went to the inspector general, making several accusations about my conduct as a commander. He then went to the group commander, stating that our monthly unit parties were nothing but slam-banging orgies with alcohol, drugs, and hookers. The group commander, Col. William McQuade, who knew better, promptly dismissed him. After all, the colonel attended our socials.

Our bridge burned; John went on his way to a new career. I went on to command the "cops" for seventeen years.

POLITICS IN GENERAL

This memory takes me to the beautiful Berkshire Mountains, just north of Springfield, Massachusetts. I lost my two businesses in 1987. A ship with no sails, I had no direction. Thirty-nine years old—and not a damn clue where my life was headed. The Air Force Reserve supplied my only income.

Then came the phone call. The 439th Military Airlift Wing, or MAW, at Westover Air Force Base was transitioning to the jumbo C5-A model transport plane. The wing needed someone to direct security during the conversion. I jumped at the temporary duty assignment, hoping there might be a full-time position at some point in the future.

For eighteen months, I managed daily operations in law enforcement and security, air shows, exercises, and even a mission during an anti-war protest. With all of my achievements, I looked forward to getting the full-time command job.

Several of my fellow officers, headed by the wing commander, General Frederick Walker, played a noontime racquetball game. I became a regular, giving me a chance to bond with the base leadership. Teams were randomly selected. I never played with the general, and my team never lost to his.

I attended a staff meeting in November 1988, quite possibly the most embarrassing day of my career. General Walker announced that Captain Robert Mooney from Dover, Delaware, would command the security forces. I was devastated. After my performance during the previous eighteen months, command overlooked me.

Speaking with my peers about the logic in the selection, I received one common response: "You've done a great job, John. But the general doesn't like to lose at racquetball."

CARL GASPAR

In the 1990s in western Pennsylvania, one transportation company stood out above all others: Carriage Limousine. My history of exceptional service landed me a position with Carriage as a chauffeur. The owners, Carl and Linda Gaspar, personally ensured that each car departed the garage in immaculate condition, driven by an experienced chauffeur who excelled in customer service.

But Carl was a paradox I never figured out. Dealing with customers, he displayed amazing charm. Dealing with drivers, the man could be ruthless.

Here are a few examples:

- As a member of the Monroeville Recreation & Parks Advisory Board in Pennsylvania, I annually oversaw the borough's Christmas light-up contest. In 1998, thinking it would be fun to drive the judges around town in a limo, I approached Carl. Realizing the marketing opportunity, he gave me a beautiful white twelve-passenger stretch, gratis. The following Saturday night, I parked my car in a spot reserved for weekday visitors. My next paycheck showed a fifty-dollar deduction for illegal parking.

- I cycled the MS 150 every June from 1996 until 2000, raising thousands of dollars for multiple sclerosis. In 1998, Carl graciously supported me with a check for one hundred dollars. My next check showed a deduction in my pay, this time for turning in a dirty vehicle—something that never happened during my almost twenty years of chauffeuring.

- Carl frequently called customers on the premise of quality control. The subject of tips always came up during the conversation. If a driver received a cash tip, Carl removed the built-in gratuity from that driver's pay.

Cash trips became the great equalizer for me. I established *arrangements* with a few hotel doormen for additional off-the-book trips in between my assigned runs. Over the years, these little bonus jobs more than compensated for Carl's actions.

Don't get mad. Get even.

JERRY MEANDERING

In 2006, I left the Air Force and transferred to the Office of Personnel Management, OPM, headquartered in an old limestone mine. The division head was a clueless manager named Jerry, who didn't get his job because of his expertise. His job was to keep his boss off his ass.

After the director approved my first assignment, the evacuation plan, Jerry only approved four of the required six golf carts needed to transport employees with special needs. This was the first time I heard him mutter, "I am the steward of the government's money."

He accompanied me on an inspection tour in Texas. A quality inspection normally took two days. He cut my first inspection to three hours—to lunch with his niece—and another inspection to sit by the hotel pool. Jerry then cut my travel time, stating I only needed three hours to complete a visit.

I was on vacation in Hawaii. OPM had only one contractor facility in Honolulu. I offered to inspect the office in exchange for two days' per diem, saving taxpayers thousands of dollars in travel expenses. He eventually performed the inspection himself over a two-week time frame.

I reserved a government vehicle for a required inspection at Fort Meade, Maryland. The *steward* caught wind of my journey and canceled the car. I was ordered to fly commercially from Pittsburgh to Baltimore. His reasoning was to save money by denying me one day's per diem. The subsequent transportation expenses cost the government over $1,500 more than if I'd driven.

I could go on about Jerry. After all, he routinely covered his ass—but none of those butts working for him. Sad part is, there are thousands of Jerrys working for the government.

MISSION ACCOMPLISHED

No one's life is perfect. HIS certainly was not. HIS out-of-control years ran from 1983 to 1996.

As a newly commissioned second lieutenant in the US Air Force, HE celebrated HIS promotion by getting stoned with HIS buddies while parked in the wing commander's parking spot at the officers' club.

HE didn't care if folks were laughing *with* HIM or *at* HIM—as long as they were laughing. When HIS commander publicly referred to HIM as "Schitt-for-brains," that attitude should have been dispelled. HE realized that too many of HIS peers laughed at HIM. A change in direction may have been necessary, but HE didn't take it.

HE flew to Vegas or drove to Atlantic City in a heartbeat to play blackjack. The bankroll didn't matter. HE was gonna conquer the world.

HE recklessly stuck HIS neck out on more than one occasion. On more than one occasion, HIS neck was almost severed.

HE had three businesses—the good, the bad, and the ugly. In the long run, it didn't matter whether they were successful or not; HE dove in anyway and lost HIS ass.

Some called HIM a free spirit.

HE often looks back on those thirteen years. You know what? If HE had a chance to take a do-over, HE'd probably do it the same way. HE developed a habit of bringing disappointments upon HIMSELF. HIS life was not always easy, but HE experienced one hell of a ride.

JOHN ROCHE

John Roche grew up in Brooklyn, New York, and moved to Pittsburgh, Pennsylvania, in 1974. He married Peggy Keaton, a western Pennsylvania redhead. John and Peggy are still married after fifty years (God bless her).

John graduated from Wagner College in Staten Island, New York, in 1973 with a BS in economics. During his college years, he drove a taxi in New York City. In 2008, he attended California University of Pennsylvania, aiming at a master's degree in homeland security. He burned out after completing only half of the program.

He retired from the US Air Force Reserve in 1996 after commanding the 911th Security Forces for seventeen years. His law enforcement career ended in 2015, when he retired from the federal Office of Personnel Management at Iron Mountain, Pennsylvania.

Between 1996 and 2014, he moonlighted as a chauffeur in Pittsburgh.

John and Peggy, both retired, live in The Villages, Florida.

Life Writers in Six-Word Memoirs

John Roche

Life Writer John Roche is well known for sleepless nights and late-night emails. On one of these nights, while we studied micro-memoir, John whipped up six-word memoirs on many of our Life Writers. Below are John's impressions of the people with whom he writes and shares his stories.

Dave. . . . . Fly high, desk jockey, *boo yah*!

Judy . . . . . Don't step in front of bus.

Steven. . . . Just too damn smart for me.

Patricia . . . Just do it—write or wrong.

Kit. . . . . . A fave of mine—Midwest charm.

Julie . . . . . Can't keep up with your moves.

Norma . . . New York, Florida, not almost heaven.

Etya . . . . . Etya, a mighty will, great glory.

Thierry . . . French soul, Québécois heart, home always.

Lucille. . . . Remember, age is just a number.

Nancy. . . . Hockey mom, my kind of girl.

Linda . . . . Farm girl with world of tails.

Raquel . . . Rookie, too new to pick on.

Terry . . . . Wish you would submit a picture.

Betty . . . . Evergreen State's contribution to Life Writers.

Sandra . . . Chair too big; Sandra too small.

Dar . . . . . Sweetest thing in whole wide world.

Jake . . . . . Come down from your perch, Jake.

Lorna . . . . Love to hear you talk, *mon.*

Holly . . . . Like Eveready bunny, keeps smiling.

Barb . . . . . Love your backdrop. Don't lean back.

Millie . . . . Sorry we were really, really bad.

Ricki . . . . Welcome back, old-timers have missed you.

Barbara . . . Crown Heights, Brooklyn, misses your charm.

Lisa Marie . Memoir? Fiction? You do it all!

Claudia . . . Miss seeing you at Colony Publix.

Jean . . . . . Writer, scrapper, genealogist—a quiet presence.

John . . . . . Surprise! Wrote this at 4:00 a.m.

Six-Word Memoirs
Life Writers

Here's a sampling of the 461 six-word memoirs written by the members of Life Writers.

Reminisce, reflect, resonate, revise, rewrite, reword . . . . .
    Kit Dwyer

I don't know where to start . . . . Dar Lamb

Bought new car, driving a computer . . . . . Norma Beasley

Spinning wind turbines above ripening corn . . . .
    Linda Peterson

Dreams should carry best by dates . . . . Lorna Deane

Never boring after I met her . . . . Dave Godin

Life is good. The alternative isn't . . . . Etya Krichmar

Getting old is not for sissies . . . . Jackie Raymond

I do not get Lady Gaga . . . . John Roche

Five-year journal, year one completed . . . . Judy Fink

Honor Society inductee never opened book . . Julie Folkerts

So hot the water looks melted . . . . Kit Dwyer

Eighty-five is really coat weather here . . . . . . John Roche

A dreaded topic yielded good stories . . . . Linda Peterson

Many times, I leaped, looked after . . . . Lorna Deane

Make time. Life is too short . . . . Julie Folkerts

Wonderful wet walrus wiggles wide whiskers . . Kit Dwyer

I love lefse Lutefisk, not much . . . . Linda Peterson

Take risks with faith, not fear . . . . Norma Beasley

Dog pals devise intruding woodchuck's demise . . . .
    Linda Peterson
Three weeks on ship, no seasickness. . Patricia Charpentier
Fifteen minutes in car, so sick . . . . . Patricia Charpentier
Birds, like bright stitches throughout life . . . . . Terry Deer
My wife is generally not amused . . . . Dave Godin
I traveled far to reach freedom . . . . Etya Krichmar
In pool, it rained. Got wet . . . . John Roche
Pencils sharpened, paper ready, already stuck . . . Judy Fink

Acknowledgments

Writing is often an isolated endeavor, but turning individual stories into a book requires the effort of many.

Thank you to all the authors who wrote, edited, and revised their stories multiple times. Your willingness to cut favorite sentences and phrases to meet the word count, oftentimes a frustrating experience, helped you all grow as writers.

Many thanks to Writing Your Life editor extraordinaire Teresa TL Bruce for your suggestions and for making our stories shine.

Thank you, Life Writer Dave Godin, for gathering and readying our photos for publication.

Thank you to Life Writer Etya Krichmar for proofreading the final manuscript.

Thank you to Joan Keyes of Dovetail Publishing Services for your creative touch in making these stories look as fabulous as they sound.

And a big thank you to Kit Dwyer for the fantastic job you did in managing this project. It was no small task, and you did it with such grace and kindness. Your dedicated efforts turned this dream into reality.

www.ingramcontent.com/pod-product-compliance
Lightning Source LLC
Chambersburg PA
CBHW070805100426
42742CB00012B/2248